SARAH FOSTER

This Is Me Smiling

To Randy:
Thank you for letting me inhabit your heart.

"I'll dream each night of some version of you

That I might not have but I did not lose ..."

"Stick Season," by Noah Kahan

Contents

Foreword

Huntington's disease worsens the ability to recognize other people's facial expressions, especially disgust. I know this from rounds of testing for the symptom as part of a long-ago HD study in Iowa. I don't believe I have encountered this symptom.

My own facial expression, I think, has been lodged in the "flat affect" straight-lipped mouth, just shy of a frown.

Recently, chorea is expressing itself through my body, and I grimace a lot without realizing or caring that I do. I have been released from normal people's habit of checking my look in the mirror.

More than anything, I sense a disconnect in moving my face to reflect happiness, or exude any emotion for that matter. It just does its own thing. My jaw, which never relaxes, is in what I like to call a "permaclench."

Burning myself, falling, aspirating beverages and runaway moods concern me more than my facial expression no longer shows others where I'm at.

Writing the memoir, "This Is Me Smiling" has been an exercise in reconstruct my relationship with my own honest emotions, especially happiness, especially joy and especially a transcendent state of peace.

After years of trying to make my dying brain solve its own mysteries, I had the epiphany that that's exactly what it's not designed to do.

I've reassigned it to seek out happiness or contentment in its simplest form.

My smile may not be visible to you, but it exists within me.

Preface

This is me, smiling

Typing has long been easier than talking, and the lessons that come with age unfold almost too quickly to capture. I didn't expect this life. Even as my grandmother, great aunt, uncle, and mother all died after wasting away from the neurodegenerative disorder Huntington's disease, I expected to beat the 50/50 odds.

Maybe you've watched the Netflix show, "Virgin River," and felt compassion for the character who knows he carries the gene for Huntington's disease. You may wonder what is in store for him, but fortunately for him, he leaves his HD at the stage door.

The film "Complete Unknown" portrays Woody Guthrie as having dementia, but doesn't reveal much about him living with HD.

I watch the show, "Shrinking," and Harrison Ford's character, who has Parkinson's, urges others to express their experiences.

It so happens that my remaining skill is explaining what I can no longer do.

If you could look through my lens in this book, I hope you can learn about HD families like mine.

I guess this is me, expressing.

Acknowledgments

Josie Hartman is responsible for this book's existence. She asked me to name 25 people whom I know love me. She printed those names on the poster, which I shared on Facebook. I have about 400 Facebook friends, and discovered it is actually cheaper to write this book than order sufficient posters and I want to leave no one out. Those friends have the last page all to themselves.

Our profound acknowledgments and gratitude for respected journalist, Taylor Sisk, a tireless helper and keeper of years of HD data. He edited this book, focusing its attention always to our family's HD, and combined my haiku chapters into real ones. He has attended many events with us, but most of all, he has been a dear and steadfast friend. I have tried to answer some of his probing questions in this book. I hope Taylor can fulfill the mission of creating the compendium of knowledge that HD deserves.

With love and gratitude to Sharon Thomason, editor, friend and a member of the organization Help4HD. Over the years, this group has provided us with guidance, information and fellowship. Sharon had the first pass at an earlier draft and may be surprised by the changes.

Thanks to my now-retired, kick-ass therapist, Rebecca B. Gaeta, for faithfully serving as my family's Giving Tree.

Thank you, Dr. Mary Edmonson, for teaching me to use the

brain I was dealt, and to express my perseverative tendencies in productive and fulfilling ways.

Thanks to everyone from HD-Reach, past and present, who has helped me so much over the years, including Sarah Dawson, Brandi Dellenback, Jared Husketh and Ann Lassiter.

With deep gratitude for everyone from the Duke Center for Movement Disorders, including, the inimitable Dr. Burton Scott, Robyn Wilson PT, Allison Allen LCSW, Kathryn Keicher, and Anne Kosem LCSW.

Thank you to Dr. Sandeep Vaishnavi and Dr. Jennifer Derr Ratley for your wisdom in caring for us.

Here in the mountains of western North Carolina, thanks to Dianne Dockery and Dr. James Jarrell at Appalachian Mountain Health Center.

From the Erlanger Outpatient Rehabilitation Center: thanks to everyone, including Speech Therapists Sandra Hogsed and Kayla; Physical Therapists Bailey Cloninger, Alex Miller, Kara Gostomski, Tiffany Totherow, and Lindsay Boharic; and Occupational Therapists Alicia Woodham and Donna O'Malley. See you again soon.

Thank you to the folks at Teva Life Effects, including Lili Radoff and Polly Brown.

Thanks to Morgan Cooke and Caroline Crowe, from ENterone. Thank you Raylene Hall.

Thank you to my lifetime friends Josie Hartman, MaryAlice Rocks Ruggiero, Rebecca Mauldin, Matt Barrett Econopoly and Leann Abdelnour.

Thank you to Susan Conley and David Beck.

Congratulations to Savannah Roberts and thanks to her and everyone at Salon El-Khouri.

Thanks to Jim and Nina McGowan; Tammy and Lonnie Biddix;

the Duggan family; Donna Gore Owens and family; Catherine and Sepp Kline; Elena and Al; Treasure, Joe and Max Dreher; and thanks to CNI and the Cherokee Scout, including David Brown.

Thanks to Rufus Wainwright, Teddy Thompson and Linda Thompson for lifting me.

Many more acknowledgments after "THE END."

Chapter 1

The Christmas gift that keeps on taking

I didn't even know what the genetic lottery meant until I lost it on Christmas Eve in 2010. That's when I learned that I had the gene that causes Huntington's disease. Here's what is in the process of happening:

Cognitive deficits will take away my ability to perform most daily tasks, but like a sick seesaw, my involuntary movement is becoming so pronounced that I won't be able to sit still or walk without dance-like movements.

Psychiatric challenges on the way include, OCD, depression, impulsive behavior, irritability, severe dementia and psychosis.

Speech becomes infrequent, labored, and inefficient.

Food eventually must be pureed and fed through a feeding tube. In the end, someone else will need do everything for me, all thanks to this incurable disease.

About a year ago, the onset of my HD kicked in. That simply means that involuntary movements have joined the party, and are starting to affect my face, hands, legs and feet. Other symptoms escalate more quickly.

The fact that I may be mistaken for someone who is drunk is

funny to 35-year-sober me.

Death from HD usually results from complications resulting from the disease, such as aspiration, starvation, cardiac issues, and wasting away. Suicide is a great risk due to the marriage of depression and impulsivity.

Even deciding to get tested has its own set of considerations. You can't unknow finding out, so unless you're emotionally prepared to know your life will change in ways you never expected, it's better to not know. The shock can forever deflate the buoyancy of hope. I had generally decided that I wanted to go on with my life, and wait to see what did or didn't happen.

I opted to test because I was concerned about difficulty with organizational, multi-tasking, and communication performance at work. I was an elementary school special education teacher in the fall of 2010 and my skills were markedly weaker than in the previous years. I could no longer make or keep track of lesson plans, so in short, I couldn't work.

All of those issues came from every angle. It seemed like I would need many specialists. At least with a diagnosis, I could get tapped into those resources.

My genetic test showed that I have a CAG repeat of 40, which meant I will definitely have HD. The next step was to find out what damage had already been done.

At Duke University, I was given a neuropsychiatric test which was a series of questionnaires and quizzes concerning a variety of cognitive skills that lasted about 3 hours. The results of this test revealed that I had extreme difficulties with tasks related to my auditory memory and visual recognition.

This kind of devastating news about a parent, I could see why someone (like Mama) may want to withhold it from their offspring. The geneticists and counselors said that my biological children needed to be informed fully, simply and soon.

So I did

The last lesson in my teaching career was me telling my own boys, "I have a brain disease called Huntington's which will make it harder for me to walk and talk. It is genetic. Your grandmother has it. You have a 50% chance of getting it."

I drew a stick figure family tree on the therapist's board.

Telling the boys was the worst and most painful thing I had ever done. I had no idea if I would still be me in five or ten years. My plan then, and now, is to live every day fully. The lie of omitting the truth of the disease often looms large and spawns its own distractions.

I was and am glad that I am still alive to write this. Since I found out about my genetic flaw in the intervening years, I have seen my kids grow up and experience life. This book is my attempt to come to terms with knowing my endgame in advance. Even though my disease onset was expected to be later than it could have been, it was forever too soon.

There is much to reckon with and much work to do in but a sliver of time.

Every genetic disease deserves a proper look back. Especially one as unusual as HD. HD can sometimes take years to go into action, so long in fact, that everyone may secretly keep their fingers crossed that it won't come or forget it is there. But when it begins, it leaves few abilities intact. Starting from the approximate top to bottoms: aspiration, choking, tooth gnashing, slurring words, biting your mouth or lips, trouble sleeping in various ways, from circadian rhythm's running opposite ways, to legs flailing, or muscles cramping.

Psychiatric issues include depression alone or with suicidal ideation, anxiety, and panic attacks. Cognitive problems limit many aspects of a person's verbal ability.

From the beginning, I have been determined to capture my HD experience. Not realizing that you have HD symptoms is actually a symptom of HD called anosognosia. I will not list the other hundreds of symptoms, but you should listen to Jimmy Pollard on YouTube for interesting lectures. He noticed, for example, that applying uneven acceleration when driving happened frequently with people he has known with HD.

Randy and I are finding, especially as we write this book, that the way we communicate about it has to be written or typed words or pictures. Verbal commands don't stick. It is knowing what adjustments to make that will help us spend more of our time as a couple. I also feel as the am the same person I have always been.

So here I am discovering how to exist in a land of repeated and differing symptoms that get worse. I will soon wear a helmet.

We are hoping this awareness of HD symptoms is a built-in super power.

When my mom's foot started writhing, I asked my dad if he noticed it.

"Yes, but I'll never say a word about it to your mother," he said. She remained unaware of the involuntary movements for years.

As Mama's disease progressed, she became paranoid and thought the water supply was poisoned. She called several local agencies repeatedly to report the poisoned water, and the confusion she must have felt was the opening that finally enabled my brother to convince her to go to UNC-Chapel Hill for an evaluation.

My mama's diagnosis of Huntington's disease was based on her presentation and family history. She refused to give a blood sample for DNA testing. She insisted that (hell no) she did not have Huntington's disease. Several doctors told her repeatedly that they were sure she did, but they were unable to convince her. Surprisingly, she actually agreed to take medicine that would lessen her severe chorea.

I told mama I was going to get tested for HD and several months later, she asked me the results of my test.

"Mama," I said, "are you sure you want to know? Do you know what it could mean?"

She said yes, so I told her that I tested positive and that is how my mom learned she had HD. When we talked, she'd say, "How's yours?" I let her know what symptoms I had and then I'd say, "How's yours?"

She always said, "I'm weak. Tired. Weak, weak, weak." My mother had just turned 80. She certainly was entitled to be tired. She had been fighting an epic battle undiagnosed, untreated, and misunderstood, just like generations of relatives before her.

In my family, HD takes its time

Part of me hoped that by the time my hard symptoms hit, I would lose my awareness, because living through HD and being fully aware of it sounds to me, like, enduring a 25 year long surgery without anesthesia. Perhaps lack of awareness was factored into the disease symptomology by the divine designer of everything, as a cruel sort of blessing. I didn't see how not knowing anything would be empowering, so I've tried over the intervening years that have made up the book you read, to face and describe each manifestation.

Eyes wide open

I want to make the road easier for Randy, for when he would need to assume the role of my caregiver.

If I could become more compliant and more reasonable (than Mama was,) I would certainly be more like me. So, visualize an awareness muscle, and am exercising it now in the hopes that the real me will be able to stick around, notice the ride. and focus on finding healthy ways to manage my symptoms.

An emotional malfunction similar to a pressure cooker is very common in HD. Once we figured out that mama had HD, I could see that Mama found herself filled with emotional pain that built up and wouldn't release on its own. When she channeled that anger at other people, her emotional load was offloaded and she felt better.

Chapter 2

Another mother

My mother, one of her former friends, Mrs. Laura Walls, once told me, was the kind of person who made a pineapple upside down cake from scratch, then drive four hours in the rain just to give it to you as your train briefly stopped at the station.

As a teenager, she climbed out of her window on hot summer nights and rode with her cousin, C.T., to the funeral home in Roseboro, where they'd sit around in the plush chairs and enjoy the air conditioning. She mastered water skiing at White Lake, and could throw off a ski and slalom. All the boys had crushes on her (confirmed decades later by the elderly town barber who went to school with her in her one stoplight home town).

She had a master's degree in music from Wake Forest. She had perfect pitch, could improvise and learn to play anything. She taught music in the city schools soon after desegregation.

That was the Mama I barely remember. The smell of her Doral cigarettes and stale, Carefree chewing gum preceded her arrival anywhere by a few moments. When she picked me up from visiting my grandparents, I would full on sob because I had saved up or postponed all of the missing of her into being upset once at the end.

That mama started crying when, sitting on her lap, I told her I had a feeling I wouldn't live very long. That mama knew about Huntington's disease and took care of everyone else in the family who had it, but never claimed it for herself or entertained any talk about having it.

My mom used to have a funny way of telling stories. Once they were having dinner with some friends in an officer's club, and one of their friends had a non-fatal heart attack. She said with all the melodrama in the world, "We had not even *touched our salads* before he was on the floor."

Accordingly, one of my maxims for minimizing was calling a situation a "crouton on the side salad of life."

By the time she was 50, she began to amass perseverative behaviors, meaning she would get stuck on things, like calling us repeatedly.

Perseveration is one of many, classic non-movement related HD symptoms that nobody knew about back then. Science may have advanced, but not in our neck of the woods. The doctors who treated the generation before mama, said HD was movement, and only movement.

But my mama had many unusual habits. She photographed the azalea bushes in her yard every week and had the film developed, but she left the envelope on the counter unopened.

When those stacks reached the ceiling, she'd throw them carelessly into a tub to spend eternity in the basement. Then she filled the counter again. There were thousands.

Her refrigerator had the same stacking ability, the refrigerator's being layers of packaged skinned, raw and discolored chicken breasts in swelling plastic that failed be liberated from the decay.

The freezer was filled with McDonalds ice cream in a cup with one bite taken and the spoon left in. Other times she ate Breyer's mint chocolate chip ice cream but spat out the chocolate pellets like they were watermelon seeds.

There was one way to do things. Her way. If you didn't take the vacuum out the right way and put the right attachment on it, your vacuuming of the floor literally ceased to exist and the dirt reappeared. She angrily vacuumed it herself and folded it back the right way in the closet.

When we helped with holiday kitchen cleanup after dinner, she criticized the way we did it, took over angrily and then was mad because she had to do it all.

She made grand, unilateral decisions that were layered with unnecessary subterfuge. For example, she secretly had a plat drawn out for a subdivision to form a mobile home park. In a separate fiscal anomaly, she paid off a loan one day and applied for another one hours later.

She flicked my brother with a dish towel to make him leave the house, but later, she'd call him incessantly at the community college where he taught.

She was Grandma Jean to my youngest son, but he called her Grandma Mean.

Mama created intricate, hateful and spiteful ways to treat our friends and spouses. One visit was all it would take for adult friends. When our spouses visited, there was always some special kind of hell she was waiting to enfold them in. She may have used an equivalent amount of planning and energy expenditure that enabled that long-ago pineapple upside down cake delivery, except now Grandma Mean was in charge. There were no labors of love. Just demands, threats, divisiveness and the insatiable need to control everyone and every action that she was aware of. Instead of Pineapple upside down cakes, she made rum cakes using a fifth of Meyers dark rum, which bolstered her popularity among some.

She kept a running list of projects that took a whole day, like going through the shed, pulling every piece out one at a time and ultimately just putting everything back where it was. I can't count the times we did that. When we offered to do it differently or on another day, she went to her list of people she overpaid to do things, and her topic of conversation was that she needed to hire them because her children weren't there for her.

Spousal abuse by proxy

Visits had to be brief. When my dad was there, he interacted with our children and spouses.

I became invested in mama just being lodged in menopause instead of having HD. I would explain away her worst behavior just to avoid facing her mounting symptoms.

I mischaracterized her motives and even her thought processes, as I mentioned, until she was gone, and until my own messed up thoughts ensued. Once we figured out that mama had HD, I could see that mama had the HD symptoms dementia communication breakdown.

The last time I saw Mama, it was late November. I went to the nursing facility and watched her sleep. She looked like an innocent doll when she slept. I tried halfheartedly to awaken her, but my body was feeling sore and I didn't want to wake her up just to say goodbye.

I'm not sure which of us I was helping, but I let her sleep. I limped and staggered outside to the car and it was windy. It didn't feel like fall anymore. It felt like winter.

Every now and then, I forget people are dead.

"My Mama is dead," I say to Randy and sometimes a tear comes out.

I try to cobble the memory bits that made up the younger, healthier and spunkier version of her.

Her brother, Uncle H.W., died before she did from HD complications. He writhed for years in a nursing home bed unless he was strapped down or given paralytic drugs.

Because the mother HD fashioned for me was the stubbornest person I've ever known, I had every idea that she would share her brother's route towards a long death bed. But I am glad she did not spend her last years that way. She was only in a nursing home for a few months and was alert most of the time.

But one day, she refused to engage in physical therapy and within weeks she contracted what we thought was a minor respiratory infection – by all accounts, her very first cold; she succumbed to it. We were surprised and unprepared. My poor brother sat for 18 hours in the nursing home with our dead mom's head in a big ice cooler, waiting in vain for researchers to take it and use it for something good. Her head was cremated with the rest of her.

I like to think she made some decision to let go, and I am glad her death wasn't due to an accident, pneumonia or heart failure. She deserved peace.

Chapter 3

My mother's mother, my would-be kidnapper, and a real-live mermaid

My mother's mother, Eva Kate, earned the name "Baboo" because she hid behind the refrigerator and jumped out at us, yelling, "Boo!" She never spoke another word to me, but she exchanged angry words with my grandfather, Hunt. Hunt's real name was Hoyt, but that sounded to us kids too much like the sound you make before you spit.

She was a statue and wore one pink house dress that my mother made for her. Her hands' daily accomplishment was working a wad of tissue into dust. The way she ate and chewed was funny to little me, and grown up me is sorry that I laughed and imitated it. She peed on the floor a lot. Standing up, once right as we were ready to leave, and my mother yelled at her.

Then she had a heart attack. In the hospital, they sat her up to feed her, and she had another heart attack and died while I was on my way to visit her. I was 16, taking my time getting to the hospital because I liked driving the new Chevette.

The receptionist took me to a room in the back where my

grandfather, Hunt, was sitting, crying uncontrollably with his false teeth sliding around and floating in a sea of slobber and tears.

Baboo was outlived by her sister, my Aunt Naomi, who lived next door to my grandparents in a brick house. Aunt Naomi, according to what my parents said when I eavesdropped from another room, was usually going bananas in one way or another.

She had shown poor judgment once by aiming her shotgun up her chimney and firing to make the hive of bees go out the top. They went down and stung her instead. Young me thought this was funny – old me does, too, if I'm being honest – and my mind replayed the incident with the bees forming an arrow, pointing at her before they set upon her and stung her.

Her depth perception was poor, and she repeatedly and accidentally stuck things in her eye. She walked into a bush with her eyes open twice. The same eye and the same bush. Part of that one eye was "false."

"How are you, shug?" was her phone greeting, and what everyone in my family used because her voice was fun to imitate. Her body never stopped moving. Even when she sat down, she had to wrap her legs around each other to keep them still. I imagined the sound of a whip wrapping around a pole.

Another aunt, a nurse named Lil, sat at Aunt Naomi's table sometimes when I visited. Like Aunt Naomi, she never had any children, but she did not act strange like her sisters. Lil didn't visit often, and when she did her attention stayed on her crossword puzzle. She seemed unusual and unfamiliar.

Young me, with the wisdom of youth, thought that she must be the unfortunate one.

Escaping a random abduction attempt

In early January of 1973, the gubernatorial inauguration was held at what (to 7-year-old me) was known as the Round Hotel. Adults knew it as the Holiday Inn hotel in Raleigh. It was shaped like a cone with a spiral parking lot below that I didn't know about because I hadn't yet seen it.

Going to the inaugural ball was the social event of the voting cycle for my family. My uncle, years later, took the girlfriend I found on the beach for him to another of those balls because he was a big fan of the big-band leaders.

He waltzed Miriam in a crowded circle around the dance floor and passed the stage just in time to make eye contact with Guy Lombardo, to whom he said, "Hi Guy!" and kept on waltzing. He could be silly like Don Knotts.

But I wouldn't meet Miriam on the beach until the next summer, so the memory returns to the one I aim to describe.

Though I was 7, I regressed when it happened. I felt nonverbal, but maybe it was from the fear. Fear put all my thoughts completely in my brain.

The reliable narrator in there would help me.

It was before the inauguration. We had just reached the hotel.

I was wearing a new dress and dressy shoes, and I was anxious because my mother must have threatened to spank me if I moved or said or did anything because we were around important people. Some of those important people wanted to have small talk with them, so they gave my brother, Rainey, the key and told us to take the elevator upstairs.

We had never taken the elevator alone, but I figured there would be no problem, since Rainey was almost three years older than me. But just before the door closed, Rainey jumped out of the elevator.

It went up a floor or two, and a man who I thought looked

like a hippie got in. He was pale and thin with messy frizzy hair and a short beard. I had never seen anyone so disheveled, and I wondered if he used drugs. He was the kind of person my mother described to scare me, a wild-eyed drug fiend. A real live bad man.

It was just me and him in the elevator and he stood too close and stared at me. Neither of us spoke, but my mind was racing. This might be one of those times in my life where something or someone could get me. I could die.

Suddenly, I had to think faster and move faster than the drug fiend. When the elevator opened several floors up, I got out. Before a hallway lined with rooms was a stairway. I ran to the stairs and started running down them. It was hard to run in my dressy shoes. The blue door at each floor led to a row of rooms like the one I had run from.

I went down about five floors and no lobby, but maybe someone could help me, and I opened the door. The same man was standing there waiting for me. I thought he had gotten out of the elevator and come looking for me.

He said, "I'm going to get you again, girl."

Silent white scream that nobody heard as I ran down a couple flights of stairs and ended up in the spiral parking garage down below the hotel. I just kept running and running down the ramp until this older couple saw me. They took me to the lobby where my mother came and got me.

Nobody in my family talked to me about the incident. Ever. Rainey didn't remember the incident but said that we didn't stay for the inauguration because my folks were too hungover from the night before.

Finding a mermaid to add to the family

The summer after second grade, I was on the beach at Surf City with my mother's brother, Uncle H.W. (pronounced dubby). Everyone but me called him Dub.

It was one of those magical times of day when everything seemed to glisten. The fish were biting, too. Mama was inside dressing the two spots and the three Virginia mullets she'd caught, and my uncle was fishing for more. I walked down a little way because I spotted an enormous amount of foam on the sand. I sat and began playing with it, rubbing the foam on my legs.

"That's how you become a mermaid," said a stranger.

Her name was Miriam. She was the easiest person in the world to talk to. She lived in Jacksonville, North Carolina, and she was a widow with three adult children. Her husband had served in World War II, Korea and Vietnam. She had a camper and spent a lot of time at the beach. Her skin was smooth and brown.

I brought the real life mermaid I found over to my uncle and they hit it off. They traveled everywhere and had their own set of friends. She became part of our family for 20 years, until Huntington's disease turned H.W. into someone who was impossibly unfamiliar and probably unsafe. Still, she came to Dub's funeral and felt like family.

Nearly drowning

A few months later, my parents invited our teachers and their families to our house for dinner at the beginning of the school year. They had never done that before or since. The kids went down to the pond behind the house. One boy, (whose name is not "Ed" but let's pretend it is. Ed was about Rainey's age and brought a fishing pole He began to fish and Rainey was nearby.

A teacher's daughter, whom I never saw before or since, was

a great swimmer and encouraged me to take a canoe out with her. She tipped it over, and we fell in. She swam easily back to shore and I started dog paddling, then I panicked because I remembered that most of the way to shore would be above my head.

I cried for help and nobody seemed to hear. They were watching Ed cast his pole out again. I had matriculated to the bobbing for my life experience. When the girl who could swim well did come to help me, I climbed her.

My dad was suddenly there and stepped through the water even though it was over his head. I began to climb him and he repeatedly threw me towards shore until I made it. He exhibited a power I only noticed once again.

Ed never did stop fishing.

The dinner party proceeded as if nobody had nearly drowned, while I sat wrapped in a towel, peeking down between the stairs at them.

When I was in trouble, I was beginning to learn, I was alone.

Grownup matters

By the fourth grade, I had not yet made a B in any class. I always told the truth and tried to be in tune with what the teachers wanted. That was my job, in my mind.

Our teacher was prone to sitting in a student's desk in front of the class and talking to us. She sat in this position when she told us about the atom bomb. She kept saying "atom bomb" in a way that let me know that she was reading something that she didn't want to read but had to read and had read it too many times. When she pulled the desk around, she usually shared something important.

A girl who was (not) named Carla was transferred into my

school part way through that year. She was a foot taller than everyone else, and she smelled like the older girls that our class stood behind in the lunch line. She was in foster care. I was afraid she could be a bully.

There was already a bully in my class that nobody knew was a bully, because her horns only came out in the girl's bathroom and the playground. Her name is only Nadine, in the telling of my experiences with her. My parents knew hers. I liked the nice, store-bought clothes she wore. I was bursting out of the last of many a blue polyester pantsuits my mom made me. She was very polite in class, but when nobody was around, like in the girl's bathroom, Nadine was a menace to others. She had it in for a sweet classmate (not) named Leigh, whose face get red when she cried. Nadine enjoyed making Leigh cry by calling her names.

One day on the playground, Nadine pushed Leigh off the monkey bars. Leigh's arm broke, and an ambulance drove behind the school and onto the playground.

Nadine told our teacher that Carla did it.

When we got inside, I noticed that Carla was gone. She didn't come back the next day, or the next.

So when the teacher, once again, pulled the desk around and sat down with us, the class was even quieter than when she told us about the atom bomb.

She told us that she knew that Carla hadn't done it, but because nobody else confessed, Carla's life was ruined. This had been her last chance before being sent to reformatory school, which my dad said was a jail for children when spankings didn't work.

The teacher told the class that she knew that some of us had seen what really happened. Someone was trying to be sly, and she had a very good idea of who wasn't talking.

I had never encountered a situation where everyone else in the room was not telling on someone. But it remained painfully quiet. Quiet that was so loud, it made me feel dizzy and lose track of the time.

They are all being quiet, I thought. Even Leigh, who had returned to school wearing a cast that nobody wanted to sign because Nadine said she had cooties. What would happen if I spoke up? Would I be sent to reformatory school? Would Nadine's parents turn the town against my parents, and would my dad lose his clients? Would I be placed in foster care? My cheeks were red and flushed, and I wanted this moment to pass. Maybe everyone knew it would stop if we didn't say anything. Maybe even more innocent people would go to reformatory school.

I said nothing. I wanted to, but I didn't. I carry that sorrow in my heart. Almost saying something didn't help Carla, and I never saw or heard about her again. No such luck with Nadine, who has continued to pop up in my periphery every now and again.

Chapter 4

A horse worth remembering

Hunt was my grandfather, and I felt so loved by him and so special. He led a team of mules through France in WWI, and his greatest memories involved foreign money he found when he went to use the bathroom.

He shared his thoughts with me about lots of topics. Sometimes, many times, more times than I could count, we talked about numbers. Hunt was always counting or keeping track of something. How many cars drove by each day. How much a quart of milk or a gallon of gas cost. How much the change in his pocket added up to.

By the time I had entered into the double digits, as we called them, I'd developed an enterprising nature. I was quick to notice that often, when we counted the change in his pocket, that change ended up with me as a gift. So we began to roll the coins together. It was an exercise in math, but for me, it was glorious, prepubescent greed. The previous year, I had gone through the "give my friends all my money" phase and been admonished by Mama for it.

I was growing into the preteen horsey phase, and, since it

intersected with my enterprising stage, I wanted to save up money to buy my own horse. My parents, as many others have since regretted, said, "If you can figure out how to make it happen, you can do it."

So, in addition to reading "Black Beauty," "All Creatures Great and Small," and young people's literature about horses, I began to read about caring for a horse from his teeth to his hoofs.

Coincidentally, Hunt's pockets and change purse began to yield exponentially larger amounts of change. The process delighted me. I rolled the loose change and had a running total for him at all times and reported to him various times of the day.

I'm pretty sure he was going by the bank, getting twenty-dollar bills broken down into coin rolls, opening the rolls, and throwing them in a change bucket that suddenly appeared. He saved the coin rollers, which I used to roll the coins for the "first" time.

Once I had rolled over $100, I started checking the local paper for ads. Several months later, I saw this: "Three-year-old green broke gelding, $329 for horse, saddle, bridle and all." A preteen expert on horse and horse gear trading prices by this time, I showed my parents. It was really up to them, because they had to find a place to board it, pay for the food, and transport me to see the horse each day.

Days later, it happened. Chief was delivered to a pasture with an old barn about a mile from home. It was hard for me to believe it happened. He smelled really good and was a good-looking horse, except he always seemed a little annoyed about something. His ears tended to lean back, and his nostrils flared.

His demeanor could have been due to the company he was

forced to keep: a 20-year-old grayed-black horse named Smokey that excelled at full body sneezes and a Shetland pony named Weasel. Weasel lived to kick other horses, and Smokey just kept to himself.

I had ridden horses at summer camp, and it was magical.

Chief had some tricks of his own. He blew up his belly every time I went about to saddle him. When I put my foot in the stirrup, he exhaled, and the saddle turned upside down.

He was a barn horse, meaning that if he caught sight of the barn, he took off for it; the barn meant that the riding was ending, and the feeding was beginning. The metaphor of a barn horse has come in handy later in life to get me to concentrate on the finish line during challenges.

When I started our ride, I pointed him the long way to the end of the pasture to keep him from seeing the barn. He learned that if he migrated towards the branches, those branches could scrape me off his back and onto the ground.

After I while, I started just hanging out with Chief. Smelling him. Patting him. Combing him. Picking his hoofs. Checking his teeth. Doing the grooming that I had read about. I never needed to ride him again. This was enough.

By the time I was in the 8th grade, I became a member of the marching band, which was an experience I had long wanted but didn't think about it interfering with the care and feeding of a horse.

My visits became "run as fast as you can and get it done." I began to leave more food and visit every other day.

This was an example of a lapse that I knew was causing a problem, but because I couldn't solve the problem, the job of solving it put on the back burner of mind, where it was forgotten. My brain was training itself to screw up. I'd remember that I was forgetting to take care of a horse, feel guilty and cry, forget about that pain by dealing, instead, with other, immediate problems.

"What are we going to do about the horse?" became the topic of conversation every so often, and that's when I cried and wailed and promised to try harder. But I still forgot, sometimes until I was in bed at night. I cried, promised to do better, but I couldn't keep up with everything. My parents, fortunately, had gotten the owner of the pasture to feed him.

Meanwhile, I joined every club in high school, had my first boyfriend, and started my life of cars, drugs and alcohol. I found out a year later that someone had come to look at Chief and bought him, horse, saddle, bridle and all.

The girl who rolled all of those coins thought she would have that horse forever, but she was wrong. Instead, she has a memory of forgetting him.

My favorite person

My dad valued the things he lacked growing up. He committed himself to having a family, living in one place and establishing a career. He went to UNC law school for two years, ran out of money and read the law during the last year, passed the bar and hung a shingle.

While he was in law school, he met Jean, and went bananas over that version of her for the rest of his life. Back then, she wore Ava Gardner red lipstick, bouffant hair with loads of hairspray that mingled with the one perfume she owned. She cooked food for other people and played the piano anywhere music was needed.

I found a box among mama's possessions containing every letter my dad had ever written to her, in order and tied up with string. He was young, exuberant and ready to tackle the world with mama.

He was a devoted husband, lawyer and father. He had a simple moral code I admired from the start: people have the same value, simple as that. In his work, everyone deserved a fair trial. Over his career, he became a lifetime criminologist, met with an FBI profiler to enrich his knowledge, and honed his specialization to help people facing death penalty charges in federal court.

In our family, we were no better (or worse) than anyone else. When my brother, a young scientist, tested this theory by telling the school bully that his dad would sue him, the bully was not the person who was reprimanded.

My dad taught me that everything can be better with a little self-deprecating humor, an unexpected, never mentioned note, an apology and a reset.

When my mom's psychiatric problems caused by HD were at full blast, my dad had a major stroke that left his long-term memory intact but his working memory reset every 12-20 minutes. For several years my mother would lose her temper because of something benign that my father had repeatedly said, like, "I saw a bird the other day."

She yelled and stormed from one room to another, held intermissions for her cigarettes, and wound down just about when nobody could take it anymore.

My dad, without fail, sheepishly said, "I saw a bird the other day." My mother would emit white hot lava.

By the next day, they had both reset and it happened again.

Icky adolescence

Like anyone growing up, I sent innocent wishes up into the

universe that I experience true love.

Students paired me with the smartest boy in class, named Bolton, for the sitting in the tree serenade. After we finished our work in third grade, I talked with Bolton about Lon Cheney, Frankenstein, and vampires. He knew a lot about every topic.

I had built up the pairing as something that was destined to happen. I had crushes on other boys, usually my brother's friends who were two years older than me. But when puberty struck in seventh grade, people were kissing and dating and talking on the phone for real.

One day, while Mr. Lucas was showing a film strip, I went all in with the yes or no letter. I held on to it while my heart raced, and my stomach growled, and my acne erupted, and until it almost disintegrated like one of Baboo's tissues, then passed it to Bolton, two rows behind.

Within moments, far too soon for contemplation, even by a smart person, to have occurred, it was back, and I opened it up. It was unchanged. Return to sender.

I should think about what other boys my age that I really liked, I told my diary, and I clipped the note to the diary and moved on. Twenty years later, I reopened that note, this time in the sharpness of daylight, and saw where someone wrote "Yes" in very, very light pencil. Mama probably found it and did that, I suspected. It was her flavor of cruel. Case in point, more than once she stole the rolling papers from my purse and left in in her bathroom closet right beside the Stayfree mini pads which we never talked about, but I used.

But I responded to the returned note at the time as a rejection. Nobody would want to pay attention to me with my oily, bumpy skin, my occasional plumpness. My hair was a frizzy mat which my Mama kept permed like hers. It left chemical burns on my skin. In fact, one day, Mr. Lucas noticed the burns and called me out in front of the class, out of concern, but it embarrassed me.

My clothes were second best preppy. I had one Dean's sweater, and one add-a-bead necklace with three, small gold beads on it. My parents had money for lessons, but never for alternate changes of clothes. So I became a lesson junky. By the time I was in high school, I was overextended and poorly dressed. The unspoken ideal then meant that you wore different sweaters every day, had necklaces full of beads, and your Levi's waist was not above 28 on the exposed tag.

In high school, those girls talked to each other and not me, except for Lee Ann Hobbs, who spoke to everyone. The boys our age talked to them and not me.

I had started staying up all night due to anxiety and skipping breakfast. I paid more attention to suppressing my stomach growling during class than to my work.

My freshman year in high school, I became the girlfriend of the only person who asked me to be. I didn't even like him, but he liked himself enough for both of us.

I was friendly with people, but could tell I made no impression on anyone. I sometimes assumed a relationship was unfolding, simply because I envisioned it. What difference would it make?

Chapter 5

Instantly alcoholic: I'll show you; I'll hurt me.

In response to any personal problem, I drank. My mantra was, "I'll show you. I'll hurt me."

I ran late to school every day, and started to hate it.

I didn't know how to play the dating game. I hated myself so much for never feeling normal enough to be asked on and go on a normal date. Upon a few occasions, I was accidentally found by a person who turned out to be kind and gentle, and I could not stop myself from sabotaging things. I was in full-on rebellion mode, and I became rigid in my beliefs, especially if they hurt others or myself.

Mama was having a nervous breakdown because she had to take care of her parents and aunt every day, providing their food and fixing Baboo's long silver hair which had never been cut. Baboo was still standing like a statue and would urinate without seeming to know that it happened.

No one needed to be cursed with me.

I felt like the mutant I was.

Boys and I ruled each other out, one after another. Then I punished myself because they were one after another. I went around that sick circle, thinking that I had boarded the wrong ship.

(The Titanic)

Young me couldn't believe what was happening, and she took away my kindness, empathy and good judgment and locked them up far away in the future.

I would have to earn them back.

By my junior year, this version of me only had a shot with boys from other high schools. For a few weeks, I could pass as normal.

One day I was stuck at a stoplight, wondering what had happened to me, when the one millionth convoy between Fort Bragg and Camp Lejeune rolled through town. Maybe my person is there, I thought.

And he was.

But I was nowhere near ready to find him.

I lived in a blackout state that was dangerous by design. The first bit of cognitive dissonance was the notion I did my best thinking when I drank. But drinking was not a good friend with which to contemplate sobriety.

On weekends, I used my fake ID to buy three six packs of beer per night for me. Once, I set out with the aim of drinking an entire pint of Everclear straight from the bottle. I passed out on my back in a parking lot, where people who hadn't quite given up on me yet rolled me over so that I would not die choking on vomit. When I was in a blackout state, the pain of my mother's wrath was absent. My brain suspended the chore of trying to figure her out.

What I thought was mama's menopause from hell, was actually the beginnings of her own inability to control her life.

When she blew, she knew exactly how to make those words hurt. She had mental folders for each of us and she adeptly drew from them.

Usually, our transgressions weren't deserving of the strength she used to propel her emotions at us. Mama, who used to let me put my head in her lap, then play with my hair, now thinks I am an insane person who should be committed. Then I left the house and smoked and drank.

My dad was escaping into scotch, and I didn't blame him. That's what I was doing. She yelled at him too, over nothing. I once made it clear to him that I wanted to live with him if they separated.

Lacking a clear head

If I somehow had a clear head, I may have understood that something was wrong with my mother, and that it could be related to something being wrong with her mother, who had Huntington's disease.

No data existed about the variability and the wide variety of HD symptoms, especially in the realm accessible to teenage me in the pre-internet world. So I made up a truth I could handle: since my grandmother was still and quiet, and my mother was the opposite, mama couldn't have HD.

But there someone went, yelling at my friends, saying disparaging things about them when they were not around, then lurking and giving me knowing looks that let me know she was about to go off on them before I could hurry them to my room or to the basement.

She stopped going to business after business and forbade me to go to them. So I rebelled against everything including mama, adult expectations and churches.

My mom slapped me and I slapped her back. I grabbed her hand to keep her from hitting me again, and squeezed her finger so hard that it hurt for the rest of her life, especially when she played the piano.

I slapped people and stayed out all night.

I adopted personal mottoes to support drinking, like, "Never, ever substitute food for alcohol." At school, if a boy glanced at me more than once in the hallway, I fabricated a relationship, and deep down, I wouldn't let go of the tiny little hope of it.

It could just be a misunderstanding, and if our paths crossed once more, or he broke up with someone else, maybe it was because he wants to go out with me. I craved the nebulous, because it was the closest I could get to intimacy.

When I wasn't in a blackout state, I was doing damage control for the things I am told I did. I had no time for school work. Memories sometime came back, but I was starting not to care about what I heard I did.

That's when my life completely lost its honest narrator.

Chapter 6

Meeting the rest of the world

The summer after my junior year, I went to the Salem College campus of Governor's School for six weeks. I immediately became friends with Leann Lysen Abdelnour, from Sparta, and she is even dearer to me today. She is a beautiful, fearless, loving and loyal.

The session included exposure to the work of composer John Cage. One of his compositions involved the pianist opening and closing the piano, almost playing, and leaving the stage. Every morning in the auditorium, as I wiped the sleep out of my eyes, I learned, at least for that morning, from people who had done a lot more thinking than me, like Charles Bukowski. Bukowski's enduring popularity, according to Adam Kirsch of The New Yorker, is due to his confessional, pulp fiction hero appeal.

My English teacher was Professor Beck. The next year, his son, David, befriended me at UNC Chapel Hill and, soon after, began to hold forth that Bob Dylan is the poet of our generation.

But our Governor's School curriculum wasn't Bob Dylan. It was African American literature, and after that summer, I

31

argued with Professor Beck's son that the poet of our generation is, in fact, Maya Angelou. We read Toni Morrison, Maya Angelou, and Malcolm X. Studying these authors and poets gave me a good foundation for further studies at UNC.

The Ebony Club was a service organization in my high school, and its members were African American. We all grew up together, and I felt loving connections with the students and particularly the advisor, Ms. Brunson.

Curious about the Ebony Club, I started going to its meetings. I felt a calmness and safety within the group, that was precious.

Looking for a fix

Six weeks at Governor's School in Winston Salem, most of it not drinking, made clear to me how fucked up my life had become. Surrounded by a campus full of overachievers, made my difficulty evident.

I wanted to fix everything, so I could have a nice, normal senior year, like this group of young adults who weren't alcoholic, didn't have my unpredictable, freak show of a mom, and didn't blank out.

I tried to patch things up with my friends, but my behavior, I know now, was dragging them down to the point that I am sure many grownups supported them when they cut me off by not responding to letters, apologies, phone calls, and messages sent through intermediaries.

For many years, I focused on the hurt of it. The fact was that we had lifetimes of friendships, and now they were gone beyond repair. I had learned my lesson, I thought, but I really hadn't. Steering clear of me was the healthiest thing for them to do. I can only understand this if I pretend that they are my own children.

32

They were young people who were not equipped to help me through any of it. Nor should they have been. I shifted my focus towards the friends I still had, like Debbie and Donna Reedy, Donna Gore, Sharon Smith, Betty Blue Caison and Eric Lewis and I am friends with most of them still.

My conscience became scarred and marred like a self-flagellating swamp dweller because I took things too far. I was out of control. Half of the classmates who elected me as senior class president wouldn't make eye contact with me or speak to me.

New to my zoo of neuroses, was blanking out entire friendships with many stable, loving supportive people. Like forgetting they exist and then not knowing how to keep remembering them. I still do it with the same people, and I can name them off, but I won't.

My senior year, my prom date was from a distant high school, a relative of a friend's boyfriend. He looked happy and kind, so the date was made.

When a limo picked me up, I was in a crisp black taffeta dress, slinky by design. My hair was short but had little Star Trek pointy sideburns. My mom took pictures in the yard with my neighbor, Donna. The whole event I had built up in my mind as something I didn't care about, but I was terrified to be around so many people who I grew up with and loved that would ignore me.

I got into the limousine, and I was nervous. "Let's have a drinking contest," I said out of nowhere. I was small then. Small like you don't realize it until you are not.

So pot was smoked, and Jack Daniels was consumed without mixer. We stopped by my date's house on the way to dinner, and I don't remember the visit at all. The blackout had already started.

The rest of the evening is pieced together from flashes of memory and what people told me. The friends that still were friends, and my family's friend, Mr. Santos, who worked at the school. I was told I started a food fight at the fancy restaurant that was also, my parents' favorite spot, and I was kicked out.

The next flash, I was getting to the prom and hanging on the date while the pictures were taken. I didn't look at those pictures for 30 years, right before I threw them out. I do vividly remember kissing a classmate's date because he was dressed up like Michael Jackson. He didn't want to be kissed.

Next, I have a flash of playing the drums on the band stand, I think, when the band took a break. Then, the last flash was poor Ms. Merritt in the hallway behind the gym. I insulted her attire in a haughty way. I was imitating my mother. I simultaneously felt possessed and trapped.

Then there's blackness for a long time. Someone drug me to the back door of my house where my father found me hours later, with my black taffeta dress pulled over my head.

Chapter 7

How Mama made the cover of Star Magazine

I got into all kinds of trouble with the school after the prom, but my parents never said a word to me about it. I white-knuckled it through the summer, not dealing with any of it, and was still able to attend UNC-Chapel Hill.

My freshman year, I lived on south campus. The walk was about three quarters of a mile down a dark and winding path with some steep spots. Already used to the walk, I was surprised when a guy asked if he could walk me there. He was charming but reserved, nice looking, and clean cut. He was the kind of boyfriend of my dreams until I met Randy. I think of him as Prelude to Randy.

We didn't get names or phone numbers; I knew enough to know that when that happens the guy isn't interested. So I went on with the semester.

Soon, I got talked into being the girlfriend of a journalism student who I wasn't attracted to mainly because his ego was disproportionately large. All of his suite mates encouraged me to take him out of the friend zone, so one Friday night, I invited him to my room, where we smoked so much pot the room seemed to be on fire.

We commenced with some kissing, and when a knock drowned the music out, he was first to the door, and he opened it. There stood the nice person, who made me feel oddly complete, the guy who walked me home. I lived on the seventh floor. I don't know how many doors he knocked on to find me. My mind was being blown.

But my new boyfriend of 10 minutes said, "She's busy, man," and closed the door on him.

I pushed it out of my mind. If that didn't deserve a voluntary blank out, nothing else did.

If you can't be with the one you love, honey, love the one you're with.

My relationship with the new boyfriend ended when he cheated on me.

Mental health crisis

Hinton James was the south campus dorm I was in. The Dean Dome would be built next door to it soon. There I medicated with alcohol, pot, beer and food. I became suicidally depressed for the first time in someone else's dorm room. For several months, I stayed up crying, not understanding what was happening or how to fix it. I played "Just the Motion" by Richard and Linda Thompson over and over, particularly the words, "It's only the pain that keeping me sane and gives me a mind to carry on," because the song, from the album, "Shoot out the Lights," was the only available stimulus that met me where I was. I might not have made it through without that song.

My pattern was: sleep in, miss class and then cry about it and smoke pot and go down the emotional abyss until sleep released me. I gained weight and started a restricted diet based on the book, "How to lose 10 pounds in two weeks." When I was heavy, I felt more invisible. To onlookers, the weight would explain my lack of a social life or, by this time, lack of initiative to even go to school.

I flunked out in the spring, and took summer classes to re enroll, but flunked out once more for the same reason. This time, I understood that I needed to work to support myself. When I wasn't around people smoking pot, I didn't seek it out, and I didn't drink at work, so times started changing for the better.

For two weeks, I worked at Darryl's restaurant. I failed to thrive there and after I dropped on the stairs a tray containing 12 frozen strawberry daiquiris made one at a time, I quit.

Around that time, I was seeing a psychiatrist, trying antide-pressants, and was suicidal enough to be committed for the first time to a psychiatric hospital, Charter Mandala in Greensboro.

My dad sent me "The Giving Tree" by Shel Silverstein.

A last hurrah

A few years later, Mama and her cousin and neighbor Sally Gale went to Ava Gardner's funeral. Sally Gale always smelled like Dentyne gum, grapefruit and nail polish. She was a daily visitor in my youth, because their yards were connected with shrubs and an iron gate. She had no children, and, without fail, still told me to leave the kitchen to let grown-ups talk. But they were lifetime best friends until HD destroyed their relationship. This may have been Mama's last hurrah.

The importance of Ava Gardner for Mama

Like Mama, Ava Gardner grew up in North Carolina. Ava

was born in Smithfield, a mere thirty-five miles from our hometown, Clinton, where nobody famous was born.

Ava Gardner's death made the cover of the Star Magazine displayed at the Piggly Wiggly checkout line. Choosing the longest line allowed Mama to secretly scan headlines, and avoid Daddy's teasing.

I happened to visit the following week. Mama summoned Sally Gale, and for the first time, she didn't ask me to leave the room. We spent hours smoking and sipping Drambuie from green glasses as they planned to crash Ava Gardner's funeral.

After Mama's second Drambuie, she admitted, between hiccups, that she was a Frank Sinatra fan instead of an Ava Gardner fan. She said that Gardner's last marriage was to Old Blue Eyes.

Gardner's autobiography, which was published posthumously revealed heartbreaking details about their relationship. Studios threatened penalties unless Gardner maintained her image and figure, so the couple terminated two pregnancies.

Mama said because Frank left his wife to marry Ava, their relationship was scandalous. I don't know if Mama was jealous of Ava's marriage to Old Blue Eyes, or disapproved of all of the divorcing. Either way I felt bad for Ava, but kept my mouth shut because I didn't want Sally Gale to tell me to leave the kitchen so grown folks could talk.

The day after Ava Gardner's funeral was my return to Chapel Hill. I wanted to hear it all to ride the levity until it ran out.

Sally Gale said, "As we entered Smithfield, Jean plunged into a conniption fit that only a glimpse of Frank Sinatra could satisfy."

Just hearing Sally Gale talk about it made Mama's face split into an enormous smile. A fleeting, goofy and joyous display.

Decades later she gave an encore when she met the handsome, honest, Young Blue Eyes, the love of my life. Frail, thin and squirmy by then, she began falling down an embankment.

Positioning, physics and bad luck aligned to show the safest way for Young Blue Eyes to catch her was by firmly grabbing her butt cheek. The notion that her rear end had just been used like a suitcase handle overrode her tendency to scowl, and allowed that impish, mischievous smile.

An instant later, it vanished. This time forever.

Sally Gale continued, "We pulled into Sunset Memorial Park in Smithfield well before anyone else. We extinguished our cigarettes out of respect for the dead."

As the press assembled, a steady rain joined the mist and ruined Mama's view. Mama's umbrella rustled, but Sally Gale didn't expect her to make a run for it. More cars arrived that were embarrassingly newer than mama's station wagon.

Then limousines with shaded windows, and the hearse arrived.

After a while, as Mama liked to tell it, "The elite neared the grave."

And so did Mama. She bolted out, leaving the passenger door open. It dinged a few times and gave up. Loud rain flooded the floor mat. She edged a step closer. Waited. Took another step. Like a rabbit in a garden pretending not to exist in the stillness.

After confirming Sinatra's absence at Ava Gardner's graveside, Mama flitted back to the car, fired up a cigarette, and was raring to go, so they were also the first to leave.

Mama's disappointment was short-lived, because despite their divorce, Old Blue Eyes loved Ava until the end. (He did.) She surmised that Old Blue Eyes must have been in one of the limousines. (He wasn't.) Regardless, the theory gave her closure. And that was the end of that. (It certainly was not.)

Mama and I had come up with a communication routine that worked. She would call me to tell me who died or was in the hospital or what my dad was up to. My dad sent me funny cards that he signed with the Mont Blanc fountain pen I gave him for Christmas.

When Dad called me in Chapel Hill, I worried, especially when he said, "I need to tell you about your mother." He had my full attention.

Cover girls

"She's OK," he said. "But her picture is right there on the cover of Star magazine this week, and she is so horrified with embarrassment that I can't get her to leave the house or talk on the phone to anyone."

Within the hour, bar customer extraordinaire Herb had fetched a stack of the magazines from Harris Teeter in exchange for tequila shots on my tab. There Mama was, featured prominently on the cover photo, under her umbrella, hanging back from the graveside. Recognizable by those who know her, but one of the "elite" for anyone else.

Mama bought up as many copies as she could find in Clinton and delivered them to the local dump. I misplaced my copies.

I never knew what unforgivable thing Mama said, but before she died Sally Gale, took out the gate between the houses and planted a fast-growing tree.

My rocky road with Mama

I considered myself to be out on my own, even though my parents were paying for my orange Oldsmobile Firenza, and for my auto and health insurance. Being on my own meant that I made my own decisions. But most importantly, it meant I did not have to talk to Mama.

More than once, I had gone a year without talking to her. She had become unrecognizable as a mother, and she scared me. She had perfected the talking points in her "shame on you" communication method to destroy her bond with her daughter.

Flicking her cigarette wherever she pleased, she pranced around at 5 feet tall, and was, to say it in a benign way, a short stack of trouble.

She polluted all of my choices, hopes and ideals by judging, questioning or ignoring them. When I told her I wanted to write, she'd ride me instead about not changing the light bulbs in the living room, and, as a result (??? I know, right??) I needed to, after being commited to the asylum, return to Sampson County, take the civil service exam so I could work the rest of my life in a dreary post office with poor lighting.

She repelled my friends for sport. As proof that my descriptions aren't hyperbola, consider this: After two of my adult friends called her a bitch, and ended visits with her, I was incredibly shocked by my friends' reactions. I thought, "I can't believe she said that to my mom! Did I miss something?"

No. I had gotten used to it. That's because crazy, years before then, had become normal. I relied on my father's love especially then.

Neither Aunt Naomi nor my precious Baboo had anger or any meanness, and I considered that data to be scientific proof that Mama didn't have Huntington's disease. I had to.

Because one of the few things we knew about HD was that it didn't skip generations. If Mama didn't have it, my life would be a life worth living. My future would not be dictated by the slow death of my brain by anything other than alcohol. My children would not be at risk.

Chapter 8

Meanwhile, in Tokyo

I had begun a relationship with someone who was already planning to go work in Tokyo. I seized the opportunity to go as well, knowing that chances like that don't come around often. (That was indeed the only chance.)

I also had high hopes for my partnership because, at least temporarily, I experienced some sort of alignment.

My first night there, after the long plane ride, the walk through Ikebukuro was like suddenly being on a different planet. Pachinko Parlors, bars, lights, lit-up billboards, noise, cars, people, more lights, and every now and then, a phone booth.

I stayed nine months, and it felt like an eternity, because I suddenly valued and missed the familiar. Especially my dog, Augie, a rat terrier I left in the care of a former roommate.

Finding my place at "Place"

Early on I found a coffee shop, named Coffee Place. It was referred to as Place. My aim in Tokyo was to teach English, dabble into copy writing, explore and make money. But after I found the Place, I barely let a day go by without going there with every English language newspaper and drinking ice coffee until it closed at 3 in the afternoon.

Yoshiko owned and ran the Place, and she was about my age. She spoke really good English and Portuguese because she lived for a while in Brazil. She became a forever friend. Her friends Fusako and Megumi also became my friends. We had meals together, where they taught me to fan rice with album covers.

Wired from coffee, I drank a bottle of wine each night, usually by myself, standing on my tiny deck, my cigarette one of a thousand fireflies that swarmed the skyscrapers. I seldom saw my roommate/friend, who I accompanied to Japan. He adopted the Japanese work ethic and was always at work. I was lonely, depressed and stuck. Prisoners of Inertia had just come out and I wove the theme of isolation into my narrator. Meanwhile my mom sent me photos of the same azalea bushes every week while I was there. New photos of the same shrubs. I began to call home collect and she'd accept the charges.

Communication, such as it was, was restored. It was because of her that I kept it together; she was really there for me; I wasn't accustomed to it, her version of mothering. I would see it later, one last time.

Teaching Mr. Inoue

When I lived in Tokyo, I worked and didn't work. I was depressed and drank most nights until I passed out. Pretty much the whole time, I taught private lessons to businessmen on Saturdays. The first student was a photographer for Playboy Japan, and was a stereotypical high life guy. He wore shades, had women dripping off him, and really didn't want to learn English. Some people just took lessons because the Gaijin (foreigner) was a novelty, like a human pet.

My other student, Mr. Inoue, was a fashion designer whose designs for women's underwear I never saw. I met Mr. Inoue last, often at a restaurant or bar, where we talked in English for an hour, he paid me three thousand yen, and I left.

When I told him I had decided to return to America, he began to show me Tokyo landmarks during our lessons. He went to my going away party and walked me home, and on the way, he unexpectedly laid a big fat kiss on me and said, "Never leave Japan!!"

We stood there in the street. He had it all figured out. He wanted me to pretend I was leaving and say goodbye to my travel companion, then meet him or call him instead. I was so shocked, mostly because I had mistaken his sexual preference. No time was available to explore options there, but I appreciated his kindness.

Besides, I had a plan to get back to my dog Augie.

Our joyful reunion

When I returned to Chapel Hill and reunited with Augie, we rolled on pine straw and a tick bit my nipple. I contracted Rocky Mountain spotted fever.

I had rented a couple of rooms at an enclave known as Boys Town in Chapel Hill. My roommate, Paul, set me up on the couch, because I was too sick to be left alone. People came by, viewed me and left. My parents came and stayed less than a minute, because it was a two-hour drive back to Clinton. When my mom walked into a room, her smell was more like hour-old chewing gum than cigarettes.

I watched "Raging Bull" over and over.

Megumi's escape

In a few months, Megumi, or Meg, as she preferred being called, came from Tokyo to Boys Town. Her trip served a dual purpose: she left her husband, then went far enough away that he would give up on her. Megumi once took me to her apartment an hour from Tokyo to show me a Nirvana album and ask me to explain Nirvana lyrics to her, and that was the only time I found no workarounds with the language barrier.

In Chapel Hill, she got a tattoo of a Rose-headed woman, I took her, at her request, to see Dexter Romweber play, and he was kind and gracious to her. A few years later, I learned that shortly after visiting me, Meg married an Iranian man, had a baby with a hole in its heart and they all died in a car crash in Iran.

I have ornate paper books that she made for me, that I have never gone through but think may be shiny. (See the last chapter to find out why shiny even matters).

My brain's last hurrah

I re-re-enrolled in school, this time paying my way. For the first time in forever, I was interested in learning. My brain appreciated the attention, and the sporadic reduction in alcohol. I learned a lot about writing living in Boys Town, particularly through my friendships with Paul, Taylor and Alvis. They read my papers as if my thoughts meant something, and gave me instructional feedback.

I had my own little office area out of site to the pool table and the other common areas. I listened to Paul's routine in real time. He had patient conversations with his mother who left lots of answering machine messages. He talked on the phone, grappling with ideas I still can't grasp. But they were all important, genuine. The kind of things that could save the world.

I took a creative writing class, and I was overwhelmed at my lack of ability. As usual, Paul gave me honest feedback. "Write what you know," he said. I was impatient to know that which could only come with experience. I began to change my narrative voice to approximate honesty instead of failing to write like Harry Crews or Raymond Chandler.

For my last assignment, I turned in an account of my mom going to Ava Gardner's funeral, and my teacher, Bland Simpson, liked it much better.

Every adult in their 20s, they said, can appreciate learning about the vastness of all they don't know. It was reassuring but maddening. After many years, I was playing an active role in what happened to me.

With concern, Paul said that after I had a certain amount to drink, I seemed like I had been hit with a frying pan. He had met the dissociative me. Living in Paul's world, with the Boys Town gang, I didn't want to be anywhere else. I came very close to regaining ambition, confidence in my intelligence and self-respect. All those years ago I happily worked on college papers, but always found someone to go out and drink with every night of the week. I drove myself home every night, keeping one eye closed so the double vision would stop. Every night that I drank, i.e., every night, I got drunk and vomited. Oddly, I have never been able to induce vomiting when sober.

When it was daylight and I had no work or school, I could pass for a healthy, albeit, hungover person. I was a vegetarian who used her *Moosewood Cookbook* to make Gypsy Soup and lentils.

Well, the daylight never shone for me as brightly as when Nora Bateson, who was then Taylor's girlfriend, arrived in town by train. Ebullient, beautiful and confident, wise and more than anything, kind. She created joy without knowing it. I had never met anyone so interesting and was at first poised, waiting for her to realize that I was damaged and worthy of being spurned. Instead, she befriended me. I was content just letting our auras overlap. We enjoyed doing girly things. For her it was amassing a collection of baby doll dresses that fit her perfectly. For me it was spending $300 on a pair of black boots that I wore until they fell apart. We wore platform shoes everywhere, and walked my dog, Augie, who led the way with his cropped tail. We followed his butt all over Chapel Hill.

Saving a Sarah

I went with Nora to a farm where she was filming, and my job was to hold the boom. I had no idea booms were heavy, and I took frequent brakes by the pond.

Among a group of children, a girl named Sarah began to think she was drowning. I immediately focused every drop of attention towards helping her out. I told her that it had happened to me when I was her age, and to make sure she talked about what happened with family and friends.

For the first time, life seemed to be showing me that I could resolve my own trauma if I paid attention for moments like these. I hoped so.

Happy ending on the way

Around this time, I began working at Pyewacket, locally legendary for its vegetarian fare and exceptional work environment. Many of the employees had higher education but preferred working there. I felt completely supported by every person there.

Still, I noticed that I could learn processes after much practice, but after a few weeks, I started inverting information or blanking out completely.

In another universe, I would work there still. Riding my Raleigh 3 speed, given to me by Miki Kersgard, down the middle of the quiet streets at 2 a.m.

One night, Nora and I were going to see "Damage" by Louis Malle, and stopped in the Hardback Café to see Paul, Taylor, or some other friends were there. She introduced me to someone who was drinking a Bass ale and reading a law book.

It was Lawrence. He was lovable and I loved him. We sent her a thank you note when we got together and she came to the wedding. Eager to start anew to be better versions of ourselves, Lawrence and I planned and executed a move to Atlanta, and moved around a few times.

I had thought that by moving out of Chapel Hill and the restaurant scene, I would be able to control my drinking. But my drinking controlled me. I went to the Stein Club on Peachtree alone one night and I felt old and barfly-esque.

Enter sobriety: stage right

Not long after, my friends Barbara and Phil, who were actors, got married at her mom's North Carolina goat farm. The wedding party was filled with other actors, some from renaissance fairs. Those couples danced with reckless abandon. Heartily and happily, with not a beverage among them. Just free.

I tapped myself on my shoulder, assured that I had the power to admit powerlessness. and thought, "That is the kind of life you want." To be free.

So I put the drink down forever. When living in Atlanta, fitness, gyms, yoga and training kept me grounded and physically healthy. I also began to see a psychiatrist and counselors.

49

Abridged account of the Atlanta years

I have only needed to pick up that first one white chip. For the first two years I hit at least two AA meetings per day. I met a wonderful sponsor whose anonymity I will keep, but love and admire her greatly. In 2023, I accidentally took a sip of Ouzo I wanted Randy to order so I could smell it, and she reminded me what the stakes were.

In Atlanta, I got a job at *Computer Currents* magazine as a reporter. The internet hadn't been cracked as a source of commerce, and many of my articles addressed possibilities.

During that time, my 2-and-a-half-year-old niece, Keiki, came to live with us for six months. I wanted to give my niece the attention she needed, but I couldn't do the job 100 percent if I did.

Other adults in sobriety could have several balls in the air at once. And take care of children. And do housework. And have hobbies. I could only think up enormous and disruptive home-improvement schemes that didn't improve the homes. Or I could spend time with the dogs to the exclusion of everything else.

I blanked out very important things at the magazine. For example, I never knew that I had a voicemail there and so I never checked it. Angry readers wanting to discuss the possibilities of online commerce were calling the publisher because I hadn't even acknowledged them. I chose my niece over that job, and I don't regret that decision.

Eventually, I took an active job at an animal hospital, and became friends with many people who worked there. Treasure and I had our two baby boys at the same time. Noah was ten weeks early and smaller than a beanie baby. Less than 2 years later, Ezra came into the world. I was also getting to know Jere, a lawyer who had a baby donkey and a bunch of long-haired animals who produced the fiber she spun. She's a scholar, an author, a thinker, a dreamer and an extremely dear friend.

Ezra was a late talker, and it was clearly because he was intellectually gifted. When he did speak, he counted and moved dog treats, "One, two three..."

After being medically advised that the program would help Ezra unfold, we enrolled both he and Noah in the Marietta Preschool. I told my mother on the phone, matter of factly, about the enrollment. She commenced to yell and curse at me, hang up, call back, repeat.

I may have called my dad at that point. She stopped calling and I hoped she was now being activated by something someone else was doing.

She calmed down and called me again, "Don't send them yet."

"Why?" If it was some irrational reason, I was hanging up.

"Ezra needs to talk," she said, and I could hear her smoking and wished that I smoked still and could fire up a Marlboro Light.

Before I could end the call, she blurted out, "You were molested."

That deserved a good listen. She smoked, and I grabbed the smiling baby Ezra and put him in the carrier that allowed me to wear him on my front. A little package of joyful boy.

I knew it couldn't have been the program at Fisher Drive, because I remembered so much of it.

She reminded me that before I went to the two Fisher Drive pre-K and kindergarten programs, Rainey and I were watched by a lady I'm calling here (for reasons soon made clear) Miss Chester. As mama spoke, I recalled a long, drawn out scene in

51

Miss Chester's driveway while I was probably about Ezra's age. I wasn't allowed to open the window.

I was not talking yet and my brother told mama that Mr. Chester put Vaseline on me and bounced me on his lap. Mama took me up the steep stairs, my memory resurfaced, to the doctor's office when the doctor looked at my private parts and pronounced my privates to have no overt injury. But I couldn't see Miss Chester anymore. Some memories have resurfaced about Mr. Chester, like his smell and his dark pants.

I got mama's point, and the boys began going to a Jewish preschool, which was attended by non-Jewish families as well, and was well respected. I looked in the window at Ezra learning about the world for weeks, surreptitiously. Jere brought her donkey to the school for show and tell. I can't remember names about the several moms and staff members, but I am grateful to have met them.

911

September 11 of 2001 was family day at a treatment facility in Marietta. I had been sitting in its parking lot since 8:15, because I didn't want to be late. But at the same time, I was in no hurry to get there, so I allowed myself to cry for a few minutes. At quarter to nine, I stayed in the car, and I listened to NPR, as I did every morning. A babysitter was keeping the boys and I couldn't tell them where I was going. Their lives shouldn't be disrupted until there was no other option, even though mine had gone to hell.

Reports came in about a plane hitting one of twin towers and I needed to find a TV. At the administrative building, I saw the hitting of the building. The staff made me leave, because family members weren't allowed to watch TV there. I went to the building where the meeting was starting, but stopped as soon as my eyes could find their wall-mounted TV. The other tower was hit. People were confused. Who was doing this? Were we at war?

The family meeting was beginning in the main room, and the door was open, so I found a seat. As people were literally jumping to their deaths, I read the room: The addicts who were already in the room were subsuming the tragedy in real time, to illustrate their addictions. "It's like my addiction is the plane and I am the tower," a person I didn't know said.

"That's about enough," I thought as I got up and walked out of the room and away from the marriage to Lawrence. I picked up the boys and we nested in bed for a very long time. In the grand scheme of things, I thought, we could get through this.

Chapter 9

Homecoming

Noah used to remember helping the real estate agent put the For-Sale sign in front of the house in Marietta. Noah, baby Ezra, three dogs and three cats came to Sampson County, North Carolina–my hometown. By this time, Jere was providing hospice for poor Augie, who I couldn't bear the thought of euthanizing.

My mom and I came up with a plan. Uncle H.W. was not using his house because he was in a care facility due to the advancing HD. Mama paid to get it renovated, replete with a storage shed, and I split my time between her house and Keiki's mom, Melissa's, house until it was ready to move in. Melissa and her mom, Dawn, took care of me, and helped me take care of the animals and the boys. Dawn was not in the town bitty-brigade, and Melissa and I had been close friends for a while. Her father liked to bring her all kinds of cool old cars, but the Studebaker was definitely "hers." It was a senior skip day, and she was a senior, so we took off in the Studebaker and recognized her dad's car coming our way. We both ducked so he wouldn't see us.

But getting back to Salemburg

In a few months, we had our own home. Five acres of farmland with 13 pecan trees planted by my great grandfather. The trees were familiar giants, they were alternatively creaking and wailing, and both sounds soothed me to sleep at night. I made time to practice yoga and walking meditation in the garden I planted. I harvested and ate things like bok choy. I picked up and sold pecans. I lived off blueberries that came off the trees near the back lot. Being able to always have an eye on the boys helped me get things done. It was flat, and the animals engaged them.

I painted a few landscapes with sheep and donkeys, but no more dinosaurs because they scared Noah and Ezra.

Dawn suggested I become a lateral entry teacher because there was a teacher shortage. First, I worked toward getting my college diploma. I lacked a level three language credit. I tried and failed college level French 3, tried and failed Italian 1 (twice), tried and dropped Russian (after one class), tried and failed Spanish 2 and Japanese. Nothing would stick. I called UNC to figure out how to handle it. They allowed me to do an Independent study from home about Nelson Mandela. I graduated, my diploma was backdated.

Needing the stability of health care and regular income, I took Dawn's advice and enrolled in a lateral entry teaching program. I had a modem and internet that connected me to the outside world. I was happier than ever. I wanted to be where I was. My mom's annoyance with every little thing was resurfacing, but I let it roll off my back.

A year after the divorce was final, I went outside in the field and looked up into the night sky, "I'm ready, if you want to send another one." My prayers were answered a million-fold, because I met Randy.

When Salembird met Avid Learner

Randy and I met on match.com. His familiar writing style captured my imagination. When I read his profile, my heart finally became complete. I sent him a message entitled: "You remind me of me." It was the best I could do at the time.

We exchanged long emails about ourselves on the platform, which became increasingly personal. In a few days, I knew I had to send him a picture, despite my ingrained fear of cameras and my knack for grimacing or otherwise contorting when posing. So, quickly, before I changed my mind, I had the teenager next door take a few shots of me wearing sweatpants with a mermaid on them and a plain T shirt. I perched on a wooden chair on the front porch of my uncle's farm house.

Anyway, I passed the photo test (it's the photo on the back cover of this book), and he called me. It felt like the call I had been waiting for all of my life, so of course I had the phone in my hand as I ran on the treadmill. I was so excited by the sound of his voice, that I fell off the treadmill. Proof, perhaps, that I have long had trouble multitasking.

Our first date was at a Starbucks inside a Barnes and Noble, which left me with a lifelong appreciation of the nested Starbucks model. I wore a sleeveless white and red top which I will never get rid of and capri pants. I grabbed a seat and looked up to see a very tall person walking down the aisle my way. He looked like he was about to pass on by, but he was lowering his trunk, and pointing his face, his smile, and his ice blue eyes right at me. I started to sweat and feel dizzy.

"Sarah?" he said. And that was really it for me. We walked to the counter to get coffee, and he turned to look at me at the same time a sunbeam shone through the window. All I saw was brilliance. It was the beginning of a very long and wonderful journey that wouldn't end.

Randy had no idea of this, however, but fortunately he seemed eager to get to know me, and to tell me stories about his ancestor Sarah Petty, his two sons (one of whom has a blue eye and a green eye), that job he once had selling vacuum cleaners door-to-door. I missed the sound of his voice when he concluded.

I was extraordinarily and uncharacteristically shy. So much so that I could barely look at him. I had not done courtship with sobriety or parenthood. I didn't want our date to end before I was able to spend more time with him. I had been so very shy that I needed to give myself another opportunity. So, we then took a stroll in an old, gothic graveyard that had fascinated me over the years. It had been vandalized, and Randy periodically interrupted our conversation to upright tombstones that had been knocked over.

I fell in love instantly and wanted to marry him, but I had to let him catch up. He did.

Destination found

When I met Randy, I immediately recognized him as the absolute destination of my long wandering heart, that sometimes says, "I told you he was out there."

Randy remembered guarding a building-in-progress alone one night and listening to the Fleetwood Mac song, "Sara." I like to think that I was looking up at the stars at the same time, requesting his entrance.

He is love of all loves, the friend of all friends. My partner.

We got married, had a baby, and were happy despite my mother's increasingly erratic and intrusive behavior.

Randy came from a place of honesty and unselfishness, and I wanted him to receive that from me.

I now fathom the depths of his loyalty, because I return that feeling. I put old tapes away and a new life began. When he looks at me, I still feel shy and want to look away. But when he's not looking at me, I stare at him. Still.

Even when I don't feel precious to myself, it's a great comfort to know that you feel precious to someone else. I told him about my family being riddled with HD, including the worst-case scenario, then I shared all of the faux intel I had amassed about Mama not having it because she was already foul humored. As I write this, my logic falls apart.

Randy is a gifted writer and storyteller. He is a loving and considerate friend. He had a group of friends in Fayetteville who were slightly younger than him. They met for coffee frequently. I assimilated into their plans, and Randy began visiting me in Salemburg.

We each had two boys from our previous marriages. They were all very smart and lovable, scrunchable. The boys met when we arranged to "run into them" at a game ranch that had ostriches and a duck who had lost the top part of his beak.

In the early days, we had every other weekend to ourselves to explore each other and the world. We walked and hiked for miles, enjoyed the beach, went scuba diving in the Virgin Islands, visited his parents in California, and went to his nephew's wedding at Yosemite.

As money, time and health permitted, we fought inertia and went out with different variations of our family, including Western NC. We went to DC. My friends MaryAlice Rocks Ruggiero and Rebecca Mauldin showed Randy and Mark New York City. Both women are such positive forces that I am grateful for. They found out we both had COVID, and had Panera food delivered to our door. My friend Josie Hartman loves to go to the beach, and I love to witness her enjoying the sun.

We went to visit Randy's sister, D.K., and father, H.L., in California and then in Oregon. We visited my aunts and cousins in Bakersfield. We enjoyed every family moment.

H.W.'s house and yard were a great place for the kids to run and explore. We accumulated cats. The children next door brought me a little kitten they found in a ditch. They were afraid it would die. I wore it under my shirt everywhere and we called her Lucky. I taught Lucky to jump from chair to chair, and then to jump through hula hoops.

Twice I woke up amidst warm wetness because Lucky gave birth to kittens on me. She didn't look pregnant either time. Argus, the golden retriever and Sebastian the Pekingese got loose and were both hit by the same car. Sebastian didn't make it, but Argus lived 8 more years.

Reactivation of the bitty brigade

If Spivey's Corner is the Hollerin' Capital of the world, then Clinton, North Carolina, is the gossiping capital of the universe. When I was in high school, about four mothers of my classmates kept a vast oral catalog of everything that happened to everyone. They cultivated relationships with young people and harvested rumors about anyone. Good deeds, misfortunes and mistakes were told with equal zeal, and judgment wasn't applied, it was implied.

I thought of them, collectively, as the bitty brigade.

My high school drama teacher knew I didn't match the town's dynamic and encouraged me to leave Clinton and never come back. Especially after what had happened at the prom.

I was absolutely positive that nothing could bring me back. But life happened, and back I was.

I worked at a school where many fellow employees were my classmates including Nadine, the person whom I let send Carla to reformatory school. One bitty who held a position of power over me, quickly she realized who I was, and set forth sabotaging my reputation.

The me that had returned to Clinton was sober and had undergone years of therapy and psychiatric treatment to get to a place where I could forgive myself for saying, "Let's have a drinking contest."

No one else knew about or needed to know about it. I was also the me whose uncle was dying of Huntington's disease, and whose mom was an anger machine. I was working full time with a bitty brigade founder, taking three classes, and had a six-month-old baby I had to rip myself away from each morning. The bitty brigade didn't care about extenuating circumstances. It would eventually end, I told myself. I tried harder to be likable and helpful. To assimilate.

One weekend, the brigade leader met my prom date, who apparently was alive and still smiling. When she came back to work she was wide eyed, like the cat about to eat the canary. Did he tell her how the date ended?

They sent me to the bathroom with every student while they stood there in the playground and gossiped about what happened to me. They fished for days to get me to tell the story of me being drunk at the prom, and I changed the subject and tried to be cheerful.

Finally, like a poorly written screenplay, each of them told an embarrassing story about having too much to drink. Some could not convincingly describe being drunk because they had never touched a drop.

Meanwhile, flashbacks of the night came back, stress and anxiety that I had put away in the "I can now live with myself" part of my brain.

I was there again, stapled to the event. I used mindfulness exercises and deep breathing. It was breaking through, and I could stop it at the phone booth door squeaks, the phone booth door squeaks, the phone booth door squeaks.

Finally, the direct question, "What about you, Sarah? Have you experienced anything like that?"

One powerful bitty was angry with me because of the traps that had been laid that I fell for because I started in the middle of the school year and missed orientation. Traffic duty, for example, was not at all optional as I had been assured. I agreed for the sake of my own family, my husband and children, to interview for a position at Clinton High School.

Flashbacks were beginning to fill in my thoughts

I returned to the same school that could have called my parents to pick me up, but didn't. They could have had some sort of intervention, directed me to counseling or have me committed. To the place that I don't want to remember. Even though they told me on the phone that it was unofficially filled, I needed work.

There was no way I could explain to Randy how much of a big deal this was for me. The administrator had already been told about my experience, so the whole thing itself became fodder for new flashbacks.

I wasn't surprised when there turned out to be no position available for me in the entire school system. But I believe I saw Ms. Brunson, as the superintendent and she still emoted serenity.

Fortunately, there was a county school system. I could start over, work less than a mile from our home, and have the boys in the same school. I could be fresh, try to make a good impression and cultivate some friendships. But if I steered clear of them, I wouldn't have to think and feel.

So I was holding steady, I thought, until a bus driver was hired who was related to the bitty brigade. Then it all started up again but worse.

Few days passed when I didn't pass her windowed transportation office, and she and whomever she was gossiping about me without looking up.

From then on, every day I went straight back to it. The flashbacks, the panic. The being left alone when I needed help.

Too much was going on in my life to stop and, at the time, I wasn't able to drill down far enough to learn what was setting me off. My emotions were becoming hard to handle. I started taking Xanax (the auto correct for which is Xanadu) under the supervision of my doctor. But soon every little thing, every classmate that happened to be working at the school, or somehow connected with the high school, reminded me what happened, and it ate away at all the work I had done to forgive myself and put the situation in the past.

Shifting priorities

All of the places we wanted to explore together had to wait for us to raise our children. I shifted my dreams for those special times with Randy and me to occur after our child was older. So, the romantic trips like the Alaskan cruise, the European trip, the cross-country drive could all wait could all wait until we were on better footing.

Like most families our age, our central focus became productivity. Randy is a journalist and I aspired to be a special education teacher, but sometimes, I worked with him working on SmartNews, but that's another book for later.

After Mark came, we moved to a really interesting house in Salemburg because we needed more room. H.W.'s house was still his, and it wasn't ours to build on to.

Financial stress, parenting a blended family that did not get along, and some bad communication patterns we developed led to a lot of arguing and yelling during that time. Both broke my heart. But I knew we still shared the same love that was born with a kiss in the graveyard, and nurtured with late-night visits after work.

Randy has a wonderful sense of humor. When we met, I was able to give him a run for his money. I laughed a lot back then. I understood humor instinctively and responded reflexively.

I began to see my perception of humor flatten and flatten and recede and recede day by day by day. When things started to change, I noticed I wasn't able to keep up with his humor and didn't respond at all or responded late. A lot of times Randy thought I wasn't listening or wasn't interested or, worse, that I was mad at him because of my flat affect.

I recognized that I was having more and more difficulty "getting" things and often Randy had to explain why the humorous bit is funny or tell it a different way. I decided that I would signal to him when I got the joke by saying "ha—- ha ha ha ha" but it is flat and wooden. Until I explained what I was doing, Randy thought I was laughing sarcastically.

It stings not being able to enjoy humor. Fortunately, my sense of humor is not completely gone. Things still get through sometimes and I am able to enjoy a snicker, a giggle, or an occasional belly laugh. In fact, the very first word out of Randy's mouth this morning, "Croatia" was the greatest bit of humor ever uttered. But I can't remember the joke. I am mindful of those moments and try to let the laughter echo into my soul. Because I never know when I might have the last laugh.

Rescued by New Bern

The promise of a better future and a new beginning for our family led us to New Bern, in eastern North Carolina. Randy became the editor of the New Bern newspaper and I became a teacher at an elementary school there. I was overjoyed because I would finally escape the ghost of my past.

I began teaching at an elementary school. The very first day, one of the teaching assistants there found out I was from Clinton and asked me if I knew the bitty brigade member she was related to.

Ruined things

The long, majestic bridge has been sullied by memories of the panic attacks I had on the way to work.

A shell was forming around me. Unfamiliar and unpleasant. I can't control it. I fight to break free. I cry until my eyeballs boil, then I replace the panic with despair.

I had been having trouble with my short-term memory. But there was a lot more going on there. I was far too anxious to work, and I worried that the children weren't safe with me. I was also distrustful of many of the other teachers who expressed concern about my performance, but not to me. I had planned to work there for several years, but in addition to memory problems, I frequently blurted out things without thinking of the repercussions, and I could neither organize lessons nor teach them. I created logs to record the flow of paperwork, but they confused me, so I could never ensure that I had sent or received anything.

Confusing interactions propagated like Tribbles but weren't nearly as cute.

During this time, I was beginning to have a gut feeling that I had no real place there to help the children, but wanted to contribute to their learning in some way. Because my auditory memory sucked, and I could only remember things visually, I made several visual, tactile learning tools for them. Tools they could manipulate and enjoy. That was the best of times. Things went downhill pretty fast.

One of my students was having an acute crisis, and the very helpful and experienced county administrator happened to be on campus.

"Let's pull the child's IEP," she said, "and see what changes we can make."

I was stunned when the administrator showed me an IEP that I had written for the student only months ago, which effectively and creatively addressed the very problems that student was having. Had I been implementing this IEP, the student may have been on a better path. I didn't remember addressing the problems and writing benchmark goals.

Forgetting about the IEP was not the first wake-up call, but it was the loudest. I was different than the other teachers. "What the hell is wrong with me?" I asked dear Susan, my department leader.

"Don't be so hard on yourself," she said, but I could see the underlying concern in her eyes. I decided to give myself a break, and let tomorrow be a new day.

A day.

I just wanted one normal day to prove to myself that I wasn't completely fucked up.

Instead, a student of mine told me repeatedly that his arm hurt during his time in my class, and I blanked it out. I heard him say it, but his words didn't connect to anything my brain thought was needed.

Well, the student didn't come to school the next day, but his angry dad sure did. "I can't believe you let my child sit through your class without sending them to the nurse. He had a broken arm. Why didn't you listen to him?"

I had no answer. My heart broke for that precious child and I kicked myself over and over for not noticing.

Mortification

How could I not notice a child with a broken arm? What the hell was wrong with me? It was time for medical intervention, and I needed to rule out the worst first. I decided to get tested for Huntington's disease.

An organization called HD-Reach provided all kinds of information, and I realized that I had a lot to learn about the disease. With their help, I found a geneticist in Chapel Hill who agreed to test me for Huntington's disease in early December 2010.

Chapter 10

The blood letting

I t started with a social worker at the genetic testing center. In a sterile, blank, but unforgettable room, she read my life to me from a new, thin file:

"You went to UNC, and you have worked as a freelance editor, veterinarian technician and mother. Now you are a special education teacher."

"Yeah, but I am having problems with that," I said. That was kind of an understatement.

"You have three biological children and two step children, right?" "Yep." Noah, Ezra, Mark, Blake and Cole.

"You left his one blank. What do you enjoy doing in your free time?"

"I do nothing anymore. I can't get started," I said. It used to be way different. I spent my free time running, lifting weights, doing hot yoga, walking dogs in Piedmont Park, and painting large murals that scared the kids. Now I come home from work and go straight from the car to bed and pull the covers up around me. I hide from the world.

"Everything seems so hard. So confusing," I told her.

So terrifyingly freakish. I have no idea how to begin to fix anything.

"What about at home? Your housework?"

"Randy does everything," I said. "He works a full day, then he comes home and does everything that I was supposed to have done around the house, and he makes dinner and manages the kids."

"How is your marriage?" Reality chimed in.

"I love him more with every year. He is the most honest person in the world," I said.

Here are the stakes, laid out in detail for all to review. Living with Huntington's disease, even the specter of it, is antithetical to an epic romance. It is the worst disease you've never heard of. Your brain deteriorates and you slowly lose the ability to think, control movements, swallow, and speak. As a bonus, you develop a myriad of psychiatric problems, memory impairment, and executive functioning problems. It either weakens your heart and it stops, you aspirate food and get pneumonia, or you starve to death. Any way you slice it, it kills you, unless you kill yourself first. Lots of people take that exit.

"Who in your family has had Huntington's disease?"

"My maternal grandmother and great aunt, and now my mother's brother," I said. It went way back in the family. I heard whispers that some distant relative hung himself on the clothesline in his yard rather than go through it.

"What about your mother?" she asked. That's when I started sobbing.

You know the deal by now. If my mom was not born with the gene, it is gone from our line of the family forever. I would be free.

Best of all, my children would be free

I had built a case in my head that HD spared her, so I always held on to the supposition that everything was okay with me. My mom was my "get out of hell free" card. I was so invested in her not having HD, that I couldn't or wouldn't connect the dots.

Two of those dots, right in front of me, were meanness and facetiousness—the hallmarks of the disease.

As evidence, neither precious Baboo nor Aunt Naomi were mean. They were quiet and still. Meanness must not run in our family's mutation. My mom was active, talkative, driving and always had some project going on.

But, about the time I started having memory problems, Mama's foot started moving, and the truth began to close in.

As I thought about all this stuff, I cried so hard I lost it a little bit, which sucked because the next person who came in was the psychiatrist.

"My job is to determine whether you are mentally stable enough to handle a bad answer from this test," he said.

"I've gotta have it!" I said.

"Maybe you might want to delay this test and process things a little more. There's no reason you have to take it right now," he said.

"I can't wait," I said, standing up from the chair so quickly that it slammed against the wall. It was very important that I keep it together.

"Look," he said, "I can't sign off on you getting this test today if I think your life will be endangered."

"The only way it would be endangered is if I continue not knowing."

I sat down and buried my face in my hands while he left me

69

in the room alone for a long time.

A phlebotomist came in to draw my blood.

Results day didn't have the decency to go as expected

In order for me to receive the results over the phone, a mental health professional had to be in the room with me. This was a previously established agreement, no matter what the answer was. My psychiatrist caught a last-minute flight out of town to visit his daughter and closed his office. Everyone between the phlebotomist to the technician at the only place in the country that performed the genetic test to the UNC folks had worked together to facilitate my finding out the results on Christmas Eve at the office of my psychiatrist.

It was an unexpected blow. I couldn't not know. If I didn't find out then, I'd have to wait until after the holidays and I would lose what was left of my mind. So, we called our family doctor, Dr. Derr, and she agreed to facilitate the phone call.

Randy and I went into her office.

The phone call from the geneticist came and they said that before they gave the results to the patient, it was routine for them to tell the health professional first, so Dr. Derr left the room for a while and came back in. I couldn't read her face. I'd agonized over the results for every second of the past two weeks. But here in the room with Dr. Derr, about to pick up the phone, I knew this was something that was all in my head, I was just having a nervous breakdown. I'm a hypochondriac. Every time I had consulted a doctor within the past few years ended up being nothing. It was with these comforts in mind that I answered the phone call from Chapel Hill.

"Sarah," the voice said, "I'm afraid that the results weren't what we had hoped."

And I collapsed and the rest was really a blur. They told me my CAG repeat was 40, and the lower the CAG the later it sometimes manifested in people. Dr. Derr was so supportive. Randy held me up and put me in the car, where I alternated between wailing and being catatonic.

It was the worst thing that could possibly happen and my life was over.

The bottom fell out of my world forever.

Beauty and symbolism of Avatar

Randy got me home and I slammed myself into bed so hard my head hit the headboard. I didn't speak, bathe, or move for days. I only cried. The kind of crying I had never experienced before, but have so many times since. Trying to cry myself away from something that shouldn't be there. Trying to grieve it away. Netflix was still delivering DVDs at that time, and "Avatar" had arrived. Randy played it in the background and, eventually, I started glancing up at it. Pretty soon the colors and sounds beat back the despair for a flicker of a moment.

"Play it," I said whenever it ended. My communication with Randy had been reduced to me grunting demands. He played "Avatar" for days as I watched it repeatedly. He ordered a copy for us to own, which we still have.

"Are the blue colors soothing?" asked Randy, trying to understand why this movie was the one thing that could get through to me.

"I identify with the guy who didn't have the use of his legs but could run free as an avatar."

I wished I had an avatar. A sheath or a cloak or a skin I could put on, inside of which there would be no Huntington's disease. It would instead be 100 percent me.

I guess I've spent my whole life since then trying to find one.

A mutant and a failure

I left the bed long enough to deal with the stuff I had to immediately address, like asking for referrals to specialists and making appointments. The idea of stepping back into that school terrified me and gave me panic attacks. But I had no choice. We needed the money and the benefits more than ever.

After the Christmas holiday, I went back to school and the very first day I knew couldn't make it.

I felt like the mutant I was. That school prided itself on competition among teachers that often appeared to be one-upmanship. I feared that everyone could tell I was abnormal and decided to keep their distance. Not Susan though. She and a few other teachers always had my back, and I'll never forget their kindness.

As a resource teacher, my kids came and went as usual. I kept my students calm, but they could tell something was off. I was moments away from a panic attack in front of them. A lot of these kids came from environments with untreated mental illness or had associations with trauma, so I had to keep my shit together or leave.

Throughout the morning, I called Randy. Then I thought to call the county office.

"How much service time is needed for long-term disability?" I asked.

"Five years," said the voice.

"How much service time do I have?" I asked.

"Five point two," they said.

"Are you sure?"

"Yes."

I called Randy and filled him in.

"Can you come down here and talk to the principal with me?" In a flash he was at the school and we went in to have a discussion with a principal who did not like me very much because of my performance this year. She took other people's weaknesses and troubles as personal insults if those problems impacted her. I wasn't in the habit of disliking people, but I deeply disliked the principal.

Anyway, the principal had just returned from being incapacitated from being attacked by one of my students, so the vibe between us was even worse. She knew nothing about the possibility I had a disease, so Randy brought her up to speed, including the positive result.

"So you're going to have it but you have it now? I don't understand." There was no empathy. No genuine interest. No eye contact.

"Movement's going to develop later in her life, but apparently, changes happen sooner." We were just learning about this, that all kinds of cognitive and psychiatric symptoms precede the onset.

I made a mental note to reexamine the way I saw Baboo, Aunt Naomi, H.W. and Mama.

"So what does this mean for work? How much time do you need off?"

"I need to go home," I said. "For good." They were better off without me. My students weren't getting their needs met with my performance.

I walked out of her wretched office and that stick-up-its-ass school for the last time in Randy's arms. We would figure something out.

THIS IS ME SMILING

Chapter 11

Kicking HD's ass

Ever since I tested positive for Huntington's disease, my dreams and plans for the future became null and void. I would not travel throughout the planet and experience it with Randy. Europe, South America and Greece would never see us together.

Instead I will spend my golden years facing decisions like whether I should use a feeding tube to prolong my life.

That's the thing about HD: It comes and it's not going to be pretty . I always, always, carry this in the back of my mind, even on my very best days. It's no surprise that suicide rates are higher for people with HD. I am fortunate that I was approved for testing because I was borderline suicidal at the very thought of being positive. But I was desperate to know, to put a name to whatever was invading my mind.

I didn't see any point to anything anymore. It would take me a year to come out of the deep depression that made my depressive episode in college seem like a pep rally.

It took me a couple more years before I could resume a somewhat limited daily routine.

And all the while it trails me like an unwanted echo. With every stagger and slurred sentence, it announces itself.

When I manage to simultaneously acknowledge and ignore it, I strike a balance I can live with. I accept a crappy future while I live each day fully. That means acknowledging that I let everyone down by testing positive. I ripped away my family's happy ending. My children have the certainty of being at risk.

If I were going express my current situation mathematically it would be: HD = monster = me. To rehabilitate my outlook, I needed to develop and internalize a new equation that reflected the understanding that the disease does the dirty work, not me.

Enter experts from all directions

I started going to the Duke Center for movement disorders. Dr. Burton Scott became my neurologist. Dr. Mary Edmonson helped me navigate psychiatric care. She explained what happens to the brain when a person has HD and explained that I could use Randy's prefrontal cortex. Telling Randy things became like having a portable RAM.

I began a long and productive relationship with Becky Gaeta, my kick ass therapist. I worked through some of the early childhood traumas, engaged in couples' therapy and learned how to intermittently let out grief in order to cope with HD. Randy took a front seat with me. Being the avid learner, he wanted to understand how to live with me, and communicate.

Because my disability prevented me from teaching, I took vocational training and evaluation which suggested I would be a good technical writer. In other words, I was back to doing what I enjoyed. What I was good at.

My counselor and friend Erica Latrice, who is now a celebrated motivator and inspirer, helped me with my resume, and I found a technical writing job.

The team was phenomenal. The work consisted of paying close attention and creating the same product. I still needed visuals to remind me for every term. For about three years Morgan, Caroline, Meredith and I had a perfect work relationship. They are such positive people, and were happy with my output. About halfway in, I shared my HD diagnosis with them and they were kind and accommodating. Around the time of COVID, my job ended.

Finding routines and forging friendships

We had a fulfilling run in New Bern, despite always having at least one son in puberty most of the time. I joke about that, but know that everyone did the best they could. The neighborhood we lived in was Ghent. An early suburb of New Bern, Ghent was laid out in a boulevard form that straddled the long-gone trolley tracks.

In New Bern, friends and neighbors made life wonderful. Right across the street, Bob Lane and Randy Toran secured a lifetime spot as the best neighbors in the world. They were like uncles to Mark, and were gracious and loving people.

Randy and I found every single thing that adorned our house from ReStore Warehouse in New Bern. Ari Sylvester became my friend because she was an employee at the ReStore, which was on my daily rounds.

Ari is an artist, fierce mother of two and a beater of cancer. She was so generous with her time and she hung out with me every moment our lives could intersect. A couple of years, she put up our Christmas trees and decorated them. I stopped doing Christmas trees before Mark was in high school. I stopped cooking holiday meals too. We go to a Chinese restaurant, or on Christmas Day, to Waffle House.

In New Bern, we lived in a 100-year-old house in the Ghent neighborhood. I crowdfunded for the down payment of the house, while its owners agreed to rent it to us in the meantime. One of New Bern's PR mavens, Linda Staunch, advised me to let people know about myself and my condition in videos to accompany my campaign.

I did, and soon after, I began my WordPress blog, Me and HD. I began to create a database of information about HD, sarahshdlist, which is woefully outdated now.

A couple of friends from the community, Ben Casey and Bill Hines, did a paddle for HD. We chose HD Reach to be the recipient of the proceeds.

This event and more comprise a period where, I am told, I successfully kicked HD's ass.

I had been introduced to Unity Church when I lived in Marietta, Georgia, and began to learn how to tap into its teachings and therefore connect to a source of strength. In New Bern, the nearest Unity was 40 minutes east, at Atlantic beach. We made many trips there and met dear friends including the minister, Catherine Kline, and her husband, Sepp, the storyteller. They remain intuitive and loving friends.

Whether I was working or not, getting up, getting ready and going somewhere helped keep me stable. I literally lost 100 pounds by going to Don and Susan's shake shop on one side of town, and gained it back on the other side of town at Donovan and Roxanne Zook's coffee shop which served homemade pie.

Susan, Don, Unity friends, and every member of the Zook family were all positive people whose natural inclination was to smile. They were generous and freely shared their lives and included us. We went to Two Rivers Church with the Zooks, and I fell in love with the Book of John. I was baptized and Roxanne gave me a beautiful Bible. It reaffirmed my belief that my mindset is malleable and portable. I can take positivity wherever I go.

Some experiences with depersonalization

Here's the crux of depersonalization as it appears as one of my HD symptoms. It's variable, ranging from a slight feeling of not feeling present in my body, to having a view of myself from the ceiling, all the way to ascribing my negative symptoms to an auxiliary me, who can describe it dispassionately.

When I can't stop myself and I say or do inappropriate things, the unfortunate situation can be so uncomfortable that the damage is done forever.

My therapist reminded me that I am a good person, and offered my being bothered by what I was doing as proof. She said the people who know me know it's HD.

At any rate, my quality of the behavior affects the way I interact with the family, and I sometimes find myself detached from the version of me the mutated gene causes.

She seems nothing like the real me.

Negotiating sometimes means that I issue a wail, and muster up. I have to push hard against that strange woman, so she will care, do, act and move.

But then she forgets, drops, stumbles and writhes. She pushes back harder and becomes less familiar, doing things I never would have done and leaving me feeling ashamed because who would believe that she did them instead of me?

When she is reeling in more and more of my day, I dedicate extra time for her to sleep, nap and go to bed early because me and my family were safe from her when I was asleep.

When I write, I feel more situated in Sarah. My brain is doing a familiar thing. I can turn her off that way sometimes. But so many times, she slithers through and insinuates herself anyway.

Here's another tale of depersonalization

My youngest son was coming to realize that he was the only student in his fourth-grade class who has this particular kind of mom waiting for him at home.

Trouble was, I wasn't interacting with Mark well or often. My response was often an irritable mood that hurt his feelings.

Often, I stayed home when Randy and Mark went out, just as much to keep them from having to see me having difficulty as to experience the satisfaction that I only felt when I was home.

Then one Sunday I took a 40-minute ride with my husband and son to the ocean. I sat in the car while they explored a Civil War fort and sat in the car again while they checked out an enormous barge being guided through a strip of deep water by tugboats. I hope they knew that my being there at all was an act of love.

When they returned, I enjoyed hearing about their adventures.

But then (here it comes) we went into a restaurant, which I had not done in some time and I felt depersonalized, like I was standing behind this ever-changing version of myself and watching her trying to operate outside the vacuum. Outside of the security of the familiar places, home and routine. My therapist said that I could have been depersonalizing to protect myself from something.

Maybe it was because it was the first time I knew other people could tell that there was definitely something wrong with me.

And I couldn't handle being "present" for that.

That wouldn't do, I realized. Instead, I should pull myself out of my comfortable, safe vacuum to create and activate a greater support system for my son.

I have never stopped trying with any of the boys.

Remembering shit

Here's what I have to work with: My short-term auditory memory had been destroyed. My neurologist said it was because HD had damaged my brain. Given a list of five words, I can, at times, repeat none of them. Conversations and anecdotes fade quickly.

A Facebook post mentioned that members of the media not being allowed to go somewhere. I asked Randy what could possibly be going on that would lead to such a situation. He told me that he had explained to me in great detail the entire situation in Ferguson, Missouri, earlier that morning. I had no memory of the conversation, but I believed him. I forgot entire conversations, and I suspect that I developed the problem years ago. Normally, Randy would have filled me in without missing a beat, but it was late and he was tired. He suggested I Google it. I thought this was a reasonable suggestion so I did so in the morning.

Reading about the situation in Ferguson made it stick in my brain longer. This reminded me that print and pictures didn't fade away as quickly as sounds. For the same reason, I now prefer texting and emailing my friends instead of talking to them so I could remember the information and have a record to refer to if I still forgot what they have told me. This is the new norm.

Social situations are a breeding round for awkward because I forget people's names and the conversations we've had. Since moving to New Bern, we have attended events each year with pretty much the same guest list. After five years, I still asked the same introductory small talk questions, like "Do you have kids?" Meanwhile, other people knew everything about me because they remember our previous conversations.

It feels odd, frustrating and embarrassing. I imagined that I seemed normal to people until they got past the "Hello."

I started skipping huge events, like Mumfest, and spending time instead with people who had stayed on the merry-go-round long enough for me to retain basic details about their lives, like Bob and Randy next door, including my friends Taylor, Rebecca, and MaryAlice from UNC. These friends have patiently and repeatedly answered the same questions for years. They understand my disability.

I, in turn, remember that they do.

Chapter 12

Downsizing rituals

As Thanksgiving of 2014 approached, HD was riding my back like a wild flying monkey as I once again galloped into the season of rituals.

This year, I chose not to produce a big turkey dinner and all the side dishes. I had cooked the bird and everything else for years. But this year, I couldn't envision myself planning and orchestrating the feast. I was growing more apathetic about such tasks.

My organizational skills in the kitchen had declined substantially over the past year. I regularly required help preparing simple, daily meals for the family. I often burned myself and had trouble pouring things, opening things and taking things out of the oven.

I still had to brave the crowds at my grocery store, but I came out of there without too much emotional fallout. One of the employees put all of my merchandise on the conveyor belt for me, and it spared me from getting tangled up in the process of doing that while a line of people would build behind me. I always had a list, but I decided that ignoring the crowds and paying attention to the list would take up all of my mental energy, so I just winged it, and looked around at what was there.

Randy suggested we have something fun but easy to cook so I didn't have to be in the kitchen all day. I immediately agreed and suggested we have Mexican food. None of the kids ever liked traditional Thanksgiving food anyway and we always ended up throwing most of it out.

When Randy got home from work, he made salsa. We put all the components on the buffet table and everyone built their own meal. I didn't have to worry about who didn't like what. Everyone would like something.

Apathy with perseveration riding shotgun: the Thelma and Louise of HD

It is important before you read any further in this book that you understand my characterization of apathy.

I categorize apathy as the Jedi Mind fuck of HD. It creates what I have always consider a useless byproduct: heightened self-centeredness. As if there were a need for that?

I have never wanted or yearned for apathy to unfold itself, and begin cloaking things going on around me. Maybe it would effectively be used as defense mechanism to cloak when my brain can't remember events anyway. Maybe all of this blanking out of memories nourishes the apathy that grows along with HD. Consider the following:

When external happenings seem to fall away around me, I can feel abandoned and forced to exclusively focus on my own concerns, desires and fears. What I want seems so painfully important that I can almost feel it out loud.

Conversely, picking up on someone else's experience is like leaning in to listen to a nearly inaudible whisper.

When people I care about are met with challenges of their own, I lack the skills to respond as I hope I used to, with long conversations, active listening (where I listened to them), visiting, or even just sitting with another person's pain so they wouldn't feel so alone. That seems like some sort of magic now, that I will never again access. Instead I plunder through the remaining livable bits of my own life, often oblivious to others.

If I can't see it, feel it or want it, I have difficulty recognizing, accessing and applying the normal schema that forms a healthy response. There's a technological mismatch that ensues, like static from an old TV masquerading as the internet.

Such functional disconnects cannot be mischaracterized as selfishness where I should hold myself accountable. It's simply a part of the life HD has dealt me, as connections and relationships are slipping away. Maybe, if I don't think too much about technique, I could reach into the top of my head and pull out an extroverted, empathetic and enthusiastic me.

Practical magic, right?

Perseveration demands that I tell you about it repeatedly and right now. Confidentially, I think of perseveration as a sawed-off shotgun of a symptom. It lacks precision and calibration but can be a reliable tool when used reasonably.

When I perseverate, I fixate on an idea and my mind just keeps going back to it, no matter what. This causes problems if I continue to dwell on a negative event or situation, like when I found out I had HD.

Shortly after my diagnosis, Dr. Edmondson, Randy and I talked about how to best handle the enormity of this symptom that seemed intent on stealing my brainpower. She said at that time we could control it, but that later there was a good chance that I would need medication to control it.

Here's how we handled it: When I perseverate about something bad, Randy redirects or distracts me. He suggests something good that's in the same wheel house or something that I used to enjoy doing before apathy came like a thief in the night and ran off with my starter.

But generally, I now use my perseverative power for good instead of evil. Over the years, I've been able to latch on to safe and productive goals, and give myself permission to go around and around about them. It enables me to figure out solutions that are better, different or a notable in some other way.

By acknowledging it out loud when it happens, invoking it, I can have power to control it, or at least steer it. Say, I buy a balloon on a string instead of the Hindenburg.

Dr. Edmondson encouraged me to intentionally shift where my thoughts point, and that turned one of the most stubborn and harmful symptoms thrown to me by HD into a secret weapon.

It's May 1, 2025, the first day of HD awareness month.

As I reach the home stretch of getting this book done, I have let people know that I am perseverating about it. It comes up in all conversations. I never don't think about it. Therefore, I am convinced that you are all reading it now.

And thank you. Your reward is an interim equation while I continue to figure things out:

"'It' Equals Everything"

I do it wrong.

I don't do it at all.

I don't do it completely.

I don't remember how to do it anymore. I forget to do it.

I've already done it and have forgotten that I did it. I hurt myself trying to do it. I dread doing it.

I don't want people to see me try to do it.
I don't want to do it.
I wish I didn't have to do it.
I won't do it today.
I won't do it until I have to.
I won't do it until someone tells me I have to.
I still won't do it when someone tells me I have to.
I won't have the energy to do it.
I'm too upset to do it.
I can do it on another day but not this day.
I wish I had done it.
I missed out on it.
I used to enjoy doing it.
I passed up my last opportunity to do it.
Is this all there is to it?

Communication and attention

Sometimes I avoid spoken conversations because mustering up the exorbitant amount of energy needed to gather the words makes it seem not worth the effort. I am more selective about conversations I initiate as well.

I can't control when others begin to talk to me, and this brings the following challenges: I am definitely thinking about something else. I wouldn't hear the first part of what was said, because it takes a bit to realize that someone is talking to me.

By the time another person's words register with me, they are already expecting me to answer but I hadn't yet taken in anything said. While working on forming an answer to the earlier question, the speaker might make a follow-up remark. To my brain, that's the equivalent of landing on the Bankrupt spot on Wheel of Fortune. I must either stop forming my answer and listen or ignore you and keep forming my answer.

In a room with a lot of people who are talking, the din of their words competes for my attention as well.

Doing something else, like walking, when talking makes it harder for me to do either. Cooking or taking medications while listening and talking often leads me to make mistakes.

The best way to make sure I am engaged from the start is to first make eye contact with me and say, "Sarah," then count to yourself "one-Mississippi, two-Mississippi" and wait until you see my face "turn on" before you speak. That would give me time to interrupt my own thoughts and focus on what you'd said.

Sitting behind me or yelling from a different room and expecting to have a conversation with me is neither successful nor pleasant for me.

Once I was sitting forward, paying attention to what was in front of me, my breakfast, when the person behind me began a conversation with me. I couldn't tune in to a voice behind me while I was looking in front of me, and I felt lost and a little scared, like things were being announced to me instead of having two-way communication. Like Big Brother was narrating my day.

The very best practice is also the most loving one: coming over to where I am sitting so our eyes can meet.

In addition to having attention problems that impact my reception of what others say to me, sometimes I have a couple of false starts when speaking. I sputter a few words, take a deep breath and then try to pronounce the words that were waiting to come out.

My family is very patient with me, providing me with the silent time I need to find the right word.

But sometimes I become impatient with myself and ask for help finishing my sentences. I ask, "What's the word?" and they offer up some suggestions.

If I can't retrieve an utterance such as "the physical therapist's office," I can sometimes access something with similarities, in this case, "the chiropractor's office." That provides a big enough clue, along with the present context, to figure out what I mean.

This fill-in-the-blank exercise with my family, at times, feels like a game show, with everyone competing to answer correctly and quickly, as if motivated by a timer. Other times it reminds me of call-and-response rituals at church.

Sometimes, when we are all at a loss as to what I was trying to say, we come up with silly answers and make a joke out of it.

And why not have fun, if an opportunity arises? This is not a funny disease, but I am learning that humor is a great strategy to cope with daily challenges.

And we all have constant, unlimited access to free laughter.

But, let's work our way back to funny as we do a 180 and I tell you . . .

. . . how I escaped the sinkhole in the abyss

One morning in the week of Christmas 2014, I woke up feeling as if I were at the bottom of an abyss, a sinkhole had formed, and I clung to the walls of the abyss so I wouldn't be sucked down into oblivion. It was so emotionally real that it felt geographically real. This was my condition until sleep redirected me, through a series of related nightmares, to the morning.

I wondered, as I woke up, how I could still be alive. My insides felt bruised and torn. My skin, like an exoskeleton. It took all of my resolve to get up and go to the bathroom.

"Don't forget," said my husband, who had been awake for some time, "you have a meeting at 9:30."

"Go for me!" I wailed.

He had known about my slip into the abyss. There have been plenty of visits to the abyss before, so many that the darkness knows my name.

But Randy had no idea about the sinkhole. I was unable to verbalize the extent of this new emotional horror I experienced the night before. Instead I stood, paralyzed.

"You need to get up and restart your routine. Now get ready."

My eyes shot daggers at him as I pulled a hat over my unwashed hair and looked for my shoes. I was furious with him for not doing what I needed. I only gave in because the meeting was to plan a fundraiser for an HD nonprofit. The only thing greater than my stubbornness, anger and despair was my desire to see this HD event through. If it had been anything else, I would still be in the fetal position in my bed.

I had no idea how I was going to make it through the meeting without crumpling into a babbling heap. I sort of brushed my teeth and went downstairs to find my husband dressed and ready.

"I won't go instead of you," he said, "but I'll go with you."

And that's all it took. No more hopelessness or misplaced anger. Instead: peace.

He wasn't going to make me go through it alone. I've never loved him more than I did at that moment.

That is how I got out of the sinkhole. I wasn't pulled out. Randy came in and we climbed out together.

Forgetting shit and the redemption of Groundhog Day

The erosion of my writing skills began with difficulty spelling ordinary words like "except." I was spelling "damn" as "damb" and liking it better that way. Several seconds of pondering now precedes correctly spelled words that used to emanate effortlessly through my fingertips.

Every so often, my family convenes to get a sense of how I've been functioning lately. Randy and Mark noticed a new perseveration: I said "Hey" a lot, as a conversation starter or greeting, then say it moments later, forgetting that I already said it. Mark timed it a few times and reported that I said it at least 10 times in five minutes.

Maybe this was my way of reintegrating my focus towards using my mouth to communicate. My utterances beyond "hey" are often mangled, and I often accidentally use odd synonyms or words that rhyme instead of the word I wanted.

I am repeatedly surprised by bits of new (to me) information my husband shares with me, which he insists he'd already told me. I trust Randy completely, especially concerning aspects of our shared reality.

But I wonder how I could forget so much. Could I land softly on the bottom of it?

I'd been experiencing slight gyrating movements each night as I waited for sleep to come. Not severe enough to blame on anything but nervous energy. A few nights later, we were in bed watching television and my body started making strong movements without my intention or permission. I just lay there for a moment and watched it, then I told Randy, who suggested that I change positions. I did and the movements subsided, but my tears took their place.

"It's happening, isn't it? I don't want it to start," I said.

I feared the shadow of what was to come and wanted to go

find a groundhog hole and burrow my way to the bottom of it.

But if I did, I might miss a wonderful spring.

Quality of life considerations

After trying on a wardrobe of decisions on behalf of future me, I decided I would rather have a feeding tube that helped avoid choking or aspiration. That's one tiny thing I can control.

But if I was hospitalized for a non-HD-related problem, like cancer, an injury or a suicide attempt, my preferences would be different. If there's a chance for my recovery, I want all the treatment I can get, and I want to be brought back if I crash.

But if I'm on a life-support machine with a poor prognosis, I want to be unplugged and not resuscitated.

I authorize the use of humane, comfortable restraints if I become violent. Under no circumstances will I be administered paralytic drugs. I also plan to compose a letter apologizing to my future medical-care providers for my bad behavior and thanking them for helping me.

I drafted a will and was ready to copy and paste it into the template that my state uses. It took several sittings and about a quart full of tears to get that far. I just had to stop for a while. It became too personal and made everything seem real and impending. I began grieving the loss of participating "as me" in my children's futures.

Emotionally hungover

I am trying to suppress out-of-control behaviors, knowing they have hurt others. Someone described them to me as "mini-aggressions." I told that person I wanted to stop the mini-aggressions forever and learned that what I wanted was as likely as wanting the sky to be pink and waking up to a pink sky.

HD is indeed upon me, damaging my brain.

My reassuring fantasies about possibly having a kinder, gentler HD had been wiped away with my hot, salty tears.

And, always, the wondering: How long can what is left of my brain compensate for the part that is damaged, or had I passed that point already?

Lack of understanding, emotional explosions as forms of communication until we are all torn apart and tired. In cases like these, when my questions no longer make sense, I know I should grab onto the notion that none of this matters, that it is all misfiring synapses and sleep deprivation. Then I shove it all into a corner of my mind and get on with my day.

Enter Vana into everyone's heart

The convention center in New Bern was the only spot big enough for large events, like the Heart Ball and the Craven Community College community fabric awards. First there was great food, and then people were recognized and music was played for the dancers.

I looked forward to going. I loved New Bern and the happy events that celebrated its sense of community. After so many events, year after year, many faces became familiar. I liked being within smiling distance of lots of acquaintances and showing goodwill without trying to have a conversation, because I never knew how my words would come out.

But when things were winding down, I was a little disappointed that I hadn't had the chance to connect with anyone not sitting at my table. Just because I dread speaking doesn't mean I don't want to connect.

An unfamiliar face named Vana, came up to me, smiling, and said, "Sarah, I just came by to say 'Hi!'" Then she vanished. She shot off like a cork from a bottle of champagne before I could see which way she went, and Randy said he hadn't seen her at all. I was sitting all the way in the front, and we were already forming ant lines to march to our cars. It was thoughtful of her to find me. But I soon forgot her name and face. I suspected that I had probably met and talked with her a dozen times. By the way she smiled at me, I could tell that she knew I have HD, and she may have been a reader of my blog.

Vana kept coming into my life, and she became part of the family. She was game for anything. She did things that I was stuck on the launchpad with, because of apathy, like cooking and gardening. She had no motive other than generosity and love.

We had a couple of farewell parties for her. One when she moved to St. Lucia, and once when she moved to Sarasota with her husband Tim.

She aligned herself with my life at every opportunity, and she loved and respected Randy in a way that warmed my heart. When she found out she had terminal cancer, I didn't not talk to her a day after that. I was there with her on the phone and by message. I have her ashes in a little ceramic container that she arranged for, and its surrounded by crystals that she sent for that purpose. She had an incredible tattoo of a phoenix on her back. I wish I had taken a photo of it. It was her spirit animal. And she was mine.

Depression

Every bout of depression now needs an action plan with Randy, which is included below.

For me, all of the pain from a hundred horrible memories entailing every bad move or misfortune conglomerates and becomes the center of my attention.

The emotional pain is so strong that it's physical. It feels like the insides of my head are being scrubbed with steel wool. A jury of people I love but misunderstand me, proclaim my massive character flaws, or suggest I don't give a damn about my family or the world surrounding me. I am face to face with failures as a mother, a person, and even a person living with HD. Then they turn their backs on me, and I am alone and the only person who understands is Randy, because he's watched HD slither its way in. When work and demands of the world take him away, I could question the importance of my existence and wonder if the world would be better if I was gone.

I am determined to live. I'm absolutely convinced that although what I'm experiencing seems to be true, it's not.

It is the lowest of the low and I wanted to try to put it to words, but don't know that I've succeeded. I do know that now it's time for me to take care of myself.

I'm going to go to bed and do deep-breathing exercises until I fall asleep. When I wake up, most likely the reset button will have been pressed and I'll feel better. If not, I'll call my therapist.

Chapter 13

Perfecting the art of forgetting

By the spring of 2015, a lot of symptoms started to emerge. The problem that most interferes with "Life as I Knew It" is how memory loss and attention problems damage communication.

Let me count the ways until I forget what I am counting:

1. I forget things people have just said.
2. I forget the names of my neighbors and coworkers.
3. I forget entire conversations, including information the other person shares and my own observations and responses. Sometimes in the middle of a duplicate conversation, I catch it and say, "Oops, we've had this conversation before."
4. I forget decisions my family just made.
5. I reintroduce people.
6. I repeat things.
7. I keep track of life by using context clues, checking, reconfirming, reviewing, and writing it down (when possible).
8. If my husband is around, I'll use his memory.

9. When I remember what I want to say, I sometimes interrupt the conversation in progress, saying, "Sorry, but I have to get this out because I just remembered it."
10. Before I get to the end of this apology/explanation, I have often forgotten the topic.
11. When I only remember the topic, I say, for example, "I can't remember, but it has to do with medicine," or, simply, "Medicine."

The listener might suggest ideas related to medicine, such as "Are you out of medicine?" "Do you need to take your medicine?" This continues until we figure out the answer, or I just give up for a moment. Sometimes a few minutes later, I sound the Wheel of Fortune buzzer with the answer: "I spilled my medicine on the floor." It may have taken seeing the pills on the floor to bring the memory back. But sometimes I never remember what the hell I wanted to say.

When all else fails, I say, "I know you've told me many times before, but could you please tell me [an important fact that was a pivotal moment in that person's life]." Usually I got that "ahhhhh" feeling as people retold me. But sometimes they'd say, "Hey; we've discussed this several times today." But I had no idea. In fact, if I didn't trust them more than my memory, I'd say they were lying.

To provide contrast between my personality from the memory damage caused by HD, I apologized to Mark for the inconvenience and frustration of having to say things again and again. If I had the choice, it wouldn't be that way.

I explained that my memory "had a mind of its own" and told him that I really wished things could be different.

My dad's stroke made him operate on a three-minute memory loop. Randy noticed that my dad figured out who Randy was each time we visited. He made the same joke about himself: "I have CRS: Can't Remember Shit!" with an exaggerated grin of pride.

Now I have my own form of CRS, and it's up to me to deal with it. I could throw my hands up in despair. But I could, like my dad, embrace my CRS and continue to practice perfecting the art of forgetting.

Not taking care of myself

Some caregivers say their loved ones with HD faced it bravely from the start, showed strength through every phase of the journey, were gracious and tried to hold on to a healthy quality of life.

Not me.

I found out I had HD in 2010, and for a solid year I was in a deep, fearful depression. I was useless to my family; a burden, even. I couldn't see beyond my own problems to those of my family and I complained about everything. I became sedentary.

Eventually, after finding a therapist who is ass-kicking good, I pulled out of the depression, but remained sedentary and continued to medicate myself (or try to kill myself) with food.

Especially ice cream. I ballooned. I went through a bad emotional patch around Easter of 2015 and upped my ice cream intake. My cocoon grew. I was now starting to show a lot more HD symptoms, but the main visible damage had been self-inflicted. Every single person in my life has told me that there is only one thing known to slow progression of HD, and that is exercise. My best friends have offered to be exercise buddies and I've ignored them. My husband tried kindly to encourage me, but I always had an excuse, or if I didn't, I would play the

HD card. I resisted until, finally, I outgrew my fat clothes and noticed that I had to turn sideways to walk between tables at a restaurant. I was, literally, fed up.

It's hard to describe the moment of change, except to say that my therapist acted as a psychological chiropractor of sorts, and one day she said something that made me snap into a mode of action. Randy and I began to take walks through our beautiful neighborhood with its tree-lined streets. I remember the day I got the first endorphin rush I've had in years. It brought back the sense memories of living in a healthy body. One that could run five miles and do 90 minutes of Bikram yoga in the front row of a hot room. I pulled out a yoga mat and turned on YouTube. I'd gotten into the habit of consuming a lot of ice cream. One week, it was a large family-sized container a day for three days. Finally, I asked myself as I threw away an empty container, "How do you think this is going to end?" I didn't like the answer.

My wonderful sister-in-law, who I love and who knows how to be healthy, suggested a solution: Instead of eating ice cream, buy mango chunks and freeze them. It worked. The coldness on my palate was just as addictive as the ice cream. Now I am hooked on mango.

The bridge and why I didn't jump

About a mile from our house was a very long ribbon of a bridge that crosses over the Neuse River. I used to drive over it on my way to work when I worked full time, and the view of New Bern and its boats and water were a spiritual experience for me twice a day.

One night, I came up with the idea of jumping off of it.

The feeling of letting my family down churned around and around in my crying head and turned into the question of why I put them through it. I could put a stop to all of it that night, I thought, if I wanted to. And I thought of the bridge.

It was tall enough that if I jumped from it, I probably wouldn't survive. So I had a way to do it and a reason to do it: I could not bear to be where I was right then.

But I didn't jump over the bridge because I had made promises to people that I would call them before I did anything that shared the category of bridge jumping.

My therapist answered. Thank God, she answered. And she listened to why I wanted to jump off the bridge and she told me that what I was feeling, while very real, was very temporary. She told me that she couldn't talk me out of jumping over the bridge, but maybe I should wait until tomorrow and see how I felt about it. She told me to go to my family members and tell them I love them and that I'm glad they're in my life, and to go up to bed and go to sleep.

And so that's what I did. I blinked and a full night of sleep had passed. It was the next morning and I didn't feel like jumping off a bridge at all. It only takes a moment of uncertainty, I realized, to jump.

Eureka, I have lost it

Paul Price wrote a song called "Vu jà dé" with the lyrics of, "I've never felt this way."

But I am up to my eyes in repeated realizations. I realize something that I think I can't un-realize but I do, and the pattern continues itself. One realization is the painful knowledge that I have already been seriously screwing with and screwing up the lives of people I love.

My renegade fear, with the precision of a jackhammer, fashioned a fully formed dystopian refugee camp, where family and friends would shelter in place in the future as HD gnawed away at my brain.

With the loyalty of a crossing guard, I direct my fears about my loved one exclusively to the future that I imagined just for them, having long ago sworn to myself that I can ready the environment so when it is time, they will have a protective realm.

I have taken some concrete steps to make amends to these folks, apologized for my own shortcomings and assured them of love.

This was a grand distraction, because my family's show had started, and it is illogical to assume that I had any control over how and when things play out.

Indeed, my periphery is already an oil spill of antics, paranoid delusions, complaints and neuroses. I have been demanding, unreasonable and impossible for years already, and am sometimes oblivious to the idea that my loved ones have already been royally screwed by me having Huntington's disease.

My complaints about every dying cell, itself, disrupts the family's normalcy. I am stunned by how I couldn't know something that was so close to me. That was created by me.

My unwanted island

That is my sliver of anosognosia. My own private island of unawareness. Could my aim be to send family there where they can magically forget all of the pain they've endured with the ease and certainty with which I forget appointments?

No, that's utter bullshit.

I have to tell you, family and friends, I see now, if only for this instant, that you've been through a worse hell than me.

Making peace with knowing

Refine my wishes. Instead of wishing for a pink sky or a cure, to wish for a healthy day.

I've wasted a lot of time wishing that I didn't know I had HD. As soon as I learned I was positive, I wished I hadn't heard. During the months that followed, when I decided whether I was going to stay in bed forever or attempt to live, I wished I didn't know.

After a decade with that knowledge, after it felt like I'd crawled on my hands and knees over shards of glass to attain some semblance of an ordinary life, I hated knowing the truth. Why? Because since I found out, I had not not thought about it. Before I tested, even with the confusion and memory loss, I was able to discern a background hum of familiar thoughts that assured me of who I was. Something that provided a backbone for the meat of living. The never-ending dream in infancy that interpreted my heartbeat as the marching of a dark army heading towards me. Then, going through a period of recognizing me and realizing that I was me and that I was a separate entity from any other entity. And later, beneath the tapes that developed through life's trials and errors, I had that base note. That bass note. That assurance that I was me. It was comforting in that it was intransigent.

Unchangeable.

Forever and ever. AMEN.

But not THE END

A new reality overtook me, all the way down to my frame. It killed my small still voice. The one so subtle that it lies underneath my inner monologue.

No understudy, no second string is waiting in the wings to

jump in and realign my sense of self. So, knowing the truth leaves me chronically uncomfortable. Like always having to wear shoes that don't fit. It sounds shrill and impatient in my head. Meditation does not stifle it. Prayer doesn't drown it. Screaming only makes it louder.

If I concede knowing is now part of my personality, there seems to be nothing I can do about it except accept that I will not live a second without being reminded by myself of the person that I really am.

In that case, there's a lot to be said for denial.

But ...

What is this "person I really am" business?

Who is the "person I really am" and what is her origin story?

I think the person I really am is me hinting that I deserve the disease because of my psychiatric or alcoholic history.

It's a part of the underlying sub- me that I don't exactly trust because of its sweeping and cautionary tone. It may be a way to, under the table, declare myself to be a monster. Those days had to stop.

I would have wondered about my symptoms either way. I already was wondering before being tested, and while I worry about symptoms now, the worrying doesn't produce nearly the stress as it did before I knew.

Too much unawareness would certainly fling my life more into my mom's collection of problems. Without recognizing that I have a disability, I couldn't have applied for the help.

I probably would have been fired from my teaching job at one place or another, if I kept my head in the sand. Aside from a few innately good people in the New Bern school, most people treated me as if I was purposely working poorly or I was lazy. Or crazy. It would be a bad scene to spill out into classrooms for everyone involved.

Without figuring out what I was dealing with, I wouldn't be in the stream of the many HD resources out there. Most significantly, I wouldn't have had the myriad of help from HD Reach, an NC nonprofit designed to help HD families connect to resources they need.

I got to meet and spend time with pioneering activists James and Ian Torrington Valvano. I met Matt Ward from Nottingham, whose videos taught me a lot about best practices and the genetics. I met people from Help4HD.

I used to rely on these organizations pretty regularly, but with every single one, I have an awkwardness and fear to go through every time I re-contact them. In each instance, I may have previously done or said something to upset the organization. I think that may be the case with HDSA national headquarters.

I used to absorb every bit of data explained by Dr. Ed Wild and Dr. Carrol when they began the HDBuzz website. I have apologized to the new folks at HDBuzz so often about things that were not upsetting to them that they recently emailed me a lifelong assurance to apply to all future occasions that I wasn't an annoyance. All reassurance helps me, especially if its written.

I have had tons of therapy and I'm taking medication that helps to control my emotional symptoms – most of the time. Anyway, I had friends. I still had my husband. So while there was the constant weight of knowing, which on a bad day seemed like an anvil, my life at the time was lighter and brighter than ever before. It was a trade-off. I couldn't not think about having HD, but that knowledge had given me my life back.

Insert one per cookie

Here's a series of HD fortune cookie fortunes that reflect my functional ability:

My fingers don't want to write, be still or pick up things.

My mouth doesn't want to speak, smile or relax.

My body doesn't want to move when it does.

My body wants to move when it doesn't.

I am losing my personality and ability to express myself.

I forgot what I did five minutes ago.

I cannot control my cravings and impulses.

I miss something so bad it hurts, but I don't know what it is. I think it's me.

Self pity

The discontent that snowballed had started early in the day, when I took my little dog to the vet. I kept nearly falling over, stumbling and side-stepping. I took a deep breath and when I exhaled I didn't tell the vet and the technician that I had HD. Instead, I just let them think what they chose to think.

It got worse when I got an email from someone I'd offered to provide administrative help to wanting to meet and talk about the arrangement. I'd been failing them. I knew they wanted to meet because of the fact that I was failing them.

I knew it wasn't not my fault. I wasn't not competent enough to do what I thought I could do. But I felt the same shame and guilt about it that I felt pre-diagnosis when I screwed things up. I revisited that place of disgusted amazement with my own inability to function and its negative impact on others, and I stayed there.

Trouble was, there was no need to stay lodged in a bad place. Was this my subreddit voice, the sub-voice that I ascribe to as a party to everything I screw up?

105

Maybe it could be a useful holding pattern until I figure things out catches up with it, like RAM and a timeout mixed together?

On this particular day, it was dinner time, and by the end of it, I was wound up tightly. I was overwhelmed and my feelings were starting to leak out. That's when we got the phone call.

Someone, a woman, had gone to the highest point of the Neuse River bridge and jumped off. That news was more than I could bear, because of the thoughts I'd had not long ago of jumping off of that same bridge. I collapsed into a sobbing blob and forced myself to go into the bedroom and take my nightly dose of tranquilizers.

Pretty soon, Randy came up to check on me and asked what I'd been thinking about when I got so upset.

I told him that I thought it was supposed to be me jumping off the bridge instead of that woman. He held me until the medication started taking effect and I'd calmed down, then he left me to rest.

Not long afterwards, Mark, who was at that time, the size of a baby impala, jumped in my bed and gave me the world's biggest hug and told me he loved me. I started blubbering again. "I am so sorry that you have to see me this way."

"That's alright," he said. "I just think about unicorns."

Coming out of a depression

Big surprises or unexpected news can send me to the edge of psychosis, before it settles as depression. It's like having a cold which always goes next to your lungs.

Whatever had gotten hold of me began to loosen its grip long enough for me to begin to let myself peek out again.

I took a long, much-needed shower. I put on clean clothes and put the clothes I had been wearing for a week in the laundry.

I went to the drugstore and bought makeup for the first time in 20 years. I bought eye liner and mascara, promising myself that I would wear it when I didn't think I might be crying. I also bought a round brush and a fat curling iron and I smoothed and curled my frizzy gray and black hair. Now I looked more like other people. Then, emboldened, I drove over to a couple of bars to pick up their music schedules for an article I was writing. As I left each bar (sober as hell) and made my way to my car, I smiled as I staggered and brushed against the other cars.

That night, my family went to another family's house for dinner. I

was a little nervous about it because I feared the topic would turn to how I'd been doing. But my son pointed out that our host had only nine toes, so maybe we could focus on that instead of my HD.

Squeezing the most out of things

It's always been the cognitive losses that scare me. I wonder, if I lose my ability to speak or communicate, how people will know when my needs and desires change? I am readying music playlist and simple art projects. I would like to make a few photo albums.

Maybe I can install a visual every day of things that I enjoyed and people that brought me happiness and push them towards my long-term memory. If I use the superpower of my perseverating mind, I can enrich ways I can have gratitude, and I will still have much in my life to be happy about. I am still head-over heels in love with my husband. All of our children were healthy and well. I live in the house that I love. My life had been enriched with more and better friendships than I ever thought possible.

I aim to wring out every last bit of flavor from each bite of ice cream, catalog each good vibe I get and otherwise absorb the happy experiences of my life. I have nothing to lose. Except the memory.

Professionals and their careers

My fair share of wonderful people has passed through my life since Huntington's disease ensnarled me. Passed through my life, like came in and helped me and left. I don't do too well when they leave. They leave for professional and family-related reasons, not because of me. But they all go.

One social worker helped me through the nightmare of testing and diagnosis and what to do then. She went away and I cried. Another social worker helped me get my disability. She worked by my side for a couple of years. Then she went away and I cried again. My psychiatrist quit practicing altogether and I still cry about that on a bad day.

Then I found out that another social worker, who had been an amazing, positive force in my life, was moving away to his happily ever after dream job. I was happy for him, but crying again.

Everybody leaves. Everybody gets to leave. Except me. I have to stay fused to HD. I cannot extricate myself for a higher paycheck, a better life or for the greater good. Spoiled me finds ways to resent all of those people who have left. How dare they not be stuck here with me! How dare they have a means and an opportunity to escape! How dare they leave me alone.

But I know I'm not alone. I have my family and friends who deserve to be treasured. And I do treasure them. I guess if I could boil it all down to something tangible, I'd wish HD was my job too. So I could quit.

Contentment and peace approaching with no popcorn

True contentment will entail not being bothered by my HD symptoms. No part of me he been removed or reassembled. I'm well rested. I've stopped poisoning my body with unhealthy food. And I'll soon see a bunch of people who I love. This has lasted for a string of days now, and I'm holding onto it as long as I can.

I've become so accustomed to describing the depths of despair, the rhythms of uncertainty and the cross hairs of the future, that it's difficult to describe these moments of precious peace, but I'll try.

It's both feeling acceptance and accepted. It's the knowledge at some point there could be no escaping any sort of trap my mind sets for itself. But I can look for troubling patterns and identify it as a construct that isn't good for me, and kick the worry down the road where forgotten things go to die. It's always returning to the joyful embrace of now, because that's where the sweetest gifts lie.

What once would have scared me now feels like a distant tickle. I'm moving through the house that I love and every window I look out of is filled with light. And every face I see or moment I imagine is a window.

Chapter 14

Moving along

My walking had begun deteriorating rapidly. I thought that since I was losing weight, it would make moving easier. And it had to some extent. But as there became less and less of me to heft around, more and more I was feeling like the scarecrow in "The Wizard of Oz." My legs went one way while my arms went another. Meanwhile, I watched to see which wall or doorway I needed to grab hold of to keep me upright or on course. The only people in the world who'd acknowledged my deterioration in this area were my sons. Mark lived with Randy and me, and seeing me stumble around was just another day in his life. "You OK?" is a phrase he'd utter a hundred times a day. Randy was permanently vigilant, responsive and never complained about anything. I was grateful and I felt loved.

My two older boys lived away from home. We'd recently been together in the North Carolina mountains after being apart for a couple of months, and I think they were a little shocked by my decline. They were never too far away from me during that or any visit. When there was a stair to climb, a hike to attempt and darkness to negotiate, one or both were there, asking me if I needed help, extending a hand or simply grabbing hold. I was grateful and I felt loved.

My two stepsons are living their best lives, all grown up and always kind to me.

Whenever we get together in any iteration, I try to say something like, "As you can see, my walking and balance are getting worse." Sometimes, people don't like to ask that kind of question. I like to get it out of the way at first, so we can know about accommodations needed. Talking about how my symptoms are helps me to better avoid avoidance and deny denial.

Whenever someone, like Vana, would walk up to me and say, "I can tell it's getting harder for you to walk. I know it must really suck." No apology is needed, I appreciate the efforts to try on my reality.

Disconnect du jour

The latest disconnect in my brain is best illustrated by the fact that one morning I used my fingers instead of utensils to fry bacon in hot grease.

The HOPES page on HD behavior symptoms has a graphic that shows how the caudate relays information to the frontal lobes. It goes like this:

Two women look in the mirror and think, "My hair is long." The one with the normal brain then thinks, "Get a haircut," while the woman with the impaired brain (me) thinks nothing about it.

That morning, to start things off, some of the plastic I'd removed from the raw bacon had fallen into the heating pan and I grabbed it out. Then I just continued to use my fingers, because they were already being used for that purpose, to arrange the raw bacon on the hot, grease-filled pan. I used my fingers to rearrange and position the bacon until hot grease was splattering on my face. So I reached into the cabinet and pulled out one of those screens that you put over chicken when it's frying. It was only at this point that the thought entered my mind that I needed to use a fork or some tongs to finish cooking the bacon.

Then, a few hours later, I had shiny fingertips where the fingerprints were less pronounced.

This behavioral disconnect plays itself out in different ways in my life. I'll walk by a piece of trash and not think that I'm supposed to pick it up. I'll see my stringy hair and not think that I need to wash it. The odd thing is, I'd known this was happening for some time, but because the part of my brain that realizes such things is not related to fixing the disconnected part of my brain, I'd continue to engage in the same risky behavior or not do things that others recognize need to be done.

Here's a handy maxim I should carry through the rest of my life: Just because I'm aware that my behavior is inappropriate doesn't mean I can alter that behavior. And no more bacon!

Recalculating reality

A person I trusted told me that I'd been manifesting depression and anxiety not as part of my symptoms but because of them.

It was hard to wrap my mind around the fact that a departure from depression and anxiety might reveal that I was functioning better than I thought. And that my brain wasn't melting.

I realize that I need to cut myself some slack and realize that living at, for example, 75 percent of my functioning capacity with a good attitude will yield a better me than freaking out over, say, 95 percent.

I began learning a little bit about what it takes to get me to do what it takes. I learned that I needed to play a bigger role in my expectations for myself. I made a schedule for myself consisting of the things I wanted to do every day that would make me happy. I was as surprised as anyone that I conjured up such a list. It's a list of things that a happy person living a good, balanced life would do every day.

It wasn't my visual reminder. It wasn't not my promise to others. It wasn't my tool for self-flagellation. It was something to work toward. I knew there were medicines that must be changed because I was still having difficulty, but I had to make the day-today success my responsibility.

Who else was going to be responsible for it?

Complaining and negativity

For several years after I tested positive for HD, I complained to anyone who would listen: "I'm not going to be able to think. I'm not going to be able to control my movements or speech." Essentially, the feedback I got was that it wasn't happening all that much then, so I might as well not think about it and focus on enjoying every day.

And I tried that, although it mostly felt like I was playing a board game on the railroad tracks. I'd captured happy moments like fireflies in a jar and stared at them until they died.

Now the stuff I was worried about happening was starting to happen, and, to be honest, I think I used up my complaining allotment. Now what I got when I shared what was going on with me was that it wasn't HD and that it happens to everybody. Every time someone said that, I wanted to vomit.

My HD, sometimes felt like driving 55 mph over 5000 miles of speed bumps with no tread on the tires and no place to pull over.

The agitated state increased the chance that my response to anything I couldn't comprehend, would resemble a defiance born from loneliness.

In the midst of this cognitive dissonance, someone asked me to write something uplifting about having HD. Unsurprisingly, that lit a fire within the hornet's nest that I have been trying to evacuate from my brain. Mustering up positivity would help positive organizations make positive change:

"Routines are important and, living with HD, I hold my routines as treasures. Eating a healthy diet, walking with my husband and even sitting covered with my favorite blanket are all simple things but, put together, they form a foundation for a life of substance. I am grateful to have some good routines in place and, when the time is right, I can plan and savor new, positive experiences. And if faced with stress, I have my routines to fall back on, to uplift me. Having healthy routines is like having a huge feather bed that I can enjoy landing on and that is always there to catch me!"

But how I felt was this:

"I am incapable of achieving anything anymore. All I can maintain are simplistic routines, and even that is hard. I can't remember processes, figure out procedures or follow written instructions. There are several things that I did last year about this time, like put up the Christmas tree and self-publish the book, that I can't seem to do now. I stumble when I walk and sometimes my legs just don't move when I tell them to. The train is coming down the tracks and all the fireflies are desiccated in the bottom of the jar. Someone please understand that this shit is happening and I do not know how to cope with it. All I can do is sit, covered in my blanket (which is an amazingly awesome blanket by the way) and wait."

So many of my friends liked on Facebook the first passage I wrote, which, at the time, I considered to be a lie. They thanked me for imparting wisdom that I lacked.

Now, I can recognize that both passages were and are true, and that's OK. That might even qualify as a step in the right direction.

Chapter 15

Getting around to sleeping

When I learned about sleep problems as an HD symptom, I didn't do much research because it seemed like small potatoes compared to the other, more blatantly hellish symptoms. I figured that sleep is the least labor-intensive thing I could do. Just close my eyes, right?

Once I had beaten every other symptom back as best as I could with cognitive therapy and handfuls of pills each day, I noticed that I was having increasing sleep difficulties, so I turned my attention towards my sleep hygiene.

According to the Stanford HOPES website regarding HD and sleep, "Because of the many detrimental effects of sleep deprivation on human health, scientists believe that the sleep disturbances associated with HD can exacerbate the disease. It goes on to say that many symptoms of sleep disorders are the same as those of HD, including the loss of motor control, memory problems, mood changes and impaired cognitive function. It's even possible that sleep deprivation is primarily responsible for some of the symptoms of HD. "This raises the interesting possibility that treating sleep problems can improve the lives of those with HD."

I'm game. Here are some problems I've had, in addition to sleep apnea, which is unrelated to HD but deserves mention here for being such a royal pain in the ass:

Difficulty falling asleep.

Difficulty staying asleep.

Difficulty going back to sleep after a trip to the bathroom.

Wiggling feet in the night.

Lack of REM sleep leading to dreamless sleep and feeling. perpetually jet lagged and ultimately never feeling rested.

Difficulty napping.

Flailing and cramping legs and arms.

Climbing out of bed while sleeping.

Yelling.

Sleep apnea causes my trigeminal neuralgia to flare up and makes me inconsistently wear a mask.

I also grind my teeth.

For a time, I saw the excellent psychiatrist, Dr. Sandeep Vaishnavi, who was based at Duke University's Preston Robert Tisch Brain Tumor Center. He is a brain expert—degenerative or otherwise. Being his patient improved my life exponentially. He gave me a sleep hygiene list, which I had seen parts of before in the wild but had never considered applying the suggestions until then.

One of the things on the list that wasn't obvious to me was that if I was having trouble sleeping, I needed to get up, go to another room, do something non-electronic and boring, like read a real paperback book, like this one (hint, hint), until I got sleepy. Then return to bed and try again. I was to repeat this several times during the night until my brain associated being in bed with the act of sleeping.

Along the same lines, I was not supposed to (gasp) watch TV in bed anymore because my brain would associate the bed with watching TV and not sleeping.

Several of my friends with HD take melatonin before bedtime, something I'd been avoiding because I took clonazepam at night. Dr. Vaishnavi assured me that it was okay to take both. The first night I took a melatonin, I arose at 5:45 a.m. ready to start the day. I've read and been told by my friends that people with HD don't produce melatonin properly or sufficiently, and I was now inclined to agree. It felt like something that was missing had been given back to me. I began looking forward to bedtime instead of dreading it.

That didn't last long. I think that melatonin products have a variability that makes it too hard for me to consistently benefit from them.

Chapter 16

My confused and guilty state

Sometimes I think there's an emotional place, very dark and very low, where only people with Huntington's disease can go. When I'm there, no medicine can placate the silent screaming I feel inside and no family member can coax or distract me from within it. I've been in and out of that particular hell so many times since the disease began its insidious arrival, wrapping itself slowly and tightly around pieces of me that used to function and squeezing the life out of them.

Much of the time I am a good soldier who marches by the lure of that hell. That hell of knowing. That hell of experiencing. I have propped myself up with so much emotional propaganda that I "pass" for being normal.

Much of the time I can take it. I make the effusive apologies for behavior and things I've forgotten and evenings I've ruined. I listen to the one hundredth remedial instruction of the proper way to do a simple household task and hope that next time I'll keep my mouth shut, maintain an accurate account of circumstances and be able to remember the instructions.

But sometimes, and this is more often the case lately, I find myself mired in a world of confusion. And that's when I feel the raw, hateful truth that it's coming for me. That's where I am now, in case you haven't guessed.

To cope until now, I've thrown pills at the crazy stuff and technology at the cognitive stuff.

Speculation has been my only method of figuring out how to meet the tag teaming of involuntary movement, cognitive issues, memory and swallowing. To do that, I get to dissociate from my future self and engage in perseverative daydreams at various speeds and ways future she could decline.

There is no "detach" option in real life though. My anticipations were all like watching movies of me. This is the real me, and I can't be a fly on my own, real wall. I'm stuck inside a body that is losing control of itself.

So, I am searching for a better way to communicate with myself about this.

Here's the thing about awareness

Unawareness that I have symptoms created by mutation of the huntingtin protein is an actual symptom.

My body applies it as a la carte symptom.

Certain things I am completely aware of. I am aware of having difficulty multitasking, remembering and speaking. I am aware of my body's involuntary movements as I write this. My feet are crossed and my ankles are playing footsie with each other. When I stop typing, my arms pull themselves down in an unnatural way and my left hand rubs the top of my leg. I pick my hand up and it joins with the other hand and interlaces the fingers.

The part of me that interacts with people has some blind

spots. I used to think they were character flaws, but, I have decided to call them HD features. Because at this stage, image is everything.

It starts out innocently enough. Sometimes I am even congratulating myself for following a routine. Feeling success in achieving complacence.

But I manage to build a wall so that I feel separate from the damage that I cause. Suddenly and unexpectedly, I do something impulsive, like buy a $2000 bed on finance while Randy is in Oregon visiting his aging father. I obsess on things that aren't important. Whatever it may be, it turns out to be the exact thing that causes disaster, as if I had been planning it for months. I do something I had promised mere hours ago to never do again. I'm listening. I'm really trying to listen. I really thought I heard it. But in truth, it takes an ice pick to chip away my wall so I can hear and register what's being said to me. Then I'm exposed and the truth: the person I love the most is choosing to have his life destroyed by me. That's not only his conscious choice for the future but what I'm doing to him now. I can't stand to be inside myself and I tell him to leave me, to let the world scoop me up and put me elsewhere – to start over and be happy.

But (thank God) he won't. He stays, and I feel guilty that I'm happy that he chooses to continue to suffer. I wish that HD could impact only me, and realize that most of the time I'm under the misapprehension that it does. Only occasionally does my wall of denial crack sufficiently to let in the truth. The disease will suck me back to oblivion before too long. The lack of awareness that's part of HD will return and I won't realize what I'm doing to the love of my life, to the most important relationship I've ever had. And it won't sting anymore because

I won't remember. But I'll keep hurting him, just the same.

Blindness that's hard to see

This lack of awareness is a blindness to how certain things i do impact Randy. It's worse than taking someone for granted. When you take someone for granted, you realize what they do for you and decide that it is not important or valuable. In my case, I forget. I forget that when I'm up, agonizing all night, he's up with me, trying everything he can to find me relief. I forget to say, first and foremost, that he's been through everything I have in an ineffably supportive nature. I forget that my bad days are his bad days. I forget that he makes the choice to inhabit this role. He could leave at any time, but he doesn't. When I remember how profoundly I disregard him, I wish he would run far away to a better life. The life he gave up so that I could have some semblance of one. This isn't what our dreams were. This is not what you deserve. The world needs to hug you. You hurt too.

Who's complacent?

It starts out innocently enough. I'm usually congratulating myself for following a routine. Feeling success in what I perceive to be my own complacence.

Maybe complacence is the very substance building a wall that separates who I think I am from the damage that I cause. Or maybe not at all.

Then I do the exact thing that causes disaster, as if I had been planning it for months. I do something I had promised mere hours ago to never do again.

I'm listening. I'm really trying to listen. I really thought I heard it. But in truth, it takes an ice pick to chip away my wall, so I can hear and register what's being said to me. Then I'm exposed and the truth stings.

Here's how the cycle plays out:

The person I love the most (Randy) is choosing to have his life destroyed by me. It's not only his conscious choice for the future but during the fallout of the latest emotional catastrophe that I created and he endured.

I can't stand to be inside my own self either and I tell him to leave me, to let the world scoop me up and put me elsewhere – to start over and be happy.

The danger of impulsivity, revisited

One day I was thinking, as I often do, about how much better it would be for people who love me if I wasn't around. Sometimes, just trying to function day to day with HD, I screw up things around me so badly that the only way I can see to make the pain and shame of it stop is to end my life. I will come back to the pain and shame part.

But then my son texted me. A troubled friend of his was faced with a crisis that ended when the friend had killed himself.

Suddenly, everything became real, and my thoughts mattered. I set aside mentally minimizing the impact my suicide would have on my children, and that was enough doubt for me on that day, to abandon any such plans.

I grieved for this poor lost child and "got it" for a little while anyway, that I should question anything my emotions insinuated.

Chapter 17

Instructional mode

By the summer of 2018, it was taking a lot of energy to understand things. For a repeated sequence of events, I needed repeated verbal instructions. Case in point: I went zip lining for the first time. After the training, I made sure I got the complete set of verbal instructions before every jump. For reasons that should seem obvious in this experience, I certainly didn't want to jump with confusion about safety. So I got the fresh message each time and I remembered long enough to get to the other side where the helper told me what to do on that side.

Memory of processes

When we got home from our mountain trip, the upstairs air conditioning wasn't working again. Randy had explained to me at least 30 times how it was supposed to work and what the problem was, but I keep cycling around to the question, "Why can't we just turn it all the way down and see if it works that way." It bothered me that I couldn't understand.

It bothered Randy because he thought he wasn't explaining

it well enough or using the right tactic, but it wasn't his fault. I just couldn't retain the concepts as they related together, and every time I bore down and tried again I felt worse about my inadequacy. I felt like I was letting him down by not retaining the information.

I wanted to give up trying to understand this one. The repair people had been called. I could bang my head all day against a wall and get a better result than spending my time trying to understand the problem.

It was just not in me anymore – the capacity to grab a concept like that and hold onto it. I determined that I would stop myself after a few reps of explanations and ask myself if the knowledge being conveyed was critical. If not, I would opt to not understand it and be happier.

We now recognize that I am having more and more difficulty "getting" things, and often Randy had to explain why the humorous bit is funny or tell it a different way.

Onset should be subjective

I started doing a do-see doe when I stopped and changed directions. It happened without me ordering my body to do it. I also started to stagger. I realized that the physical symptoms I'd been spared from until now could be developing. For some reason, that's when doctors decree that you have "onset." As if you're perfectly normal until then, which everyone knows isn't the case. But that's when the time starts being measured in terms of circling the drain. You have an expected lifespan after that.

I'd been reveling in my "this is as good as it gets" approximation of a normal, happy life, supported by lots of prescription medicine and by people who love me. But that wouldn't be enough to counterbalance what was to come if it was indeed coming. Still, as 2018 ended, I was doing extremely well in sum. I was working very hard at it. A daily, behind-the-scenes commitment to a positive outlook had helped me preserve, nay, improve my capacity.

But there also was a minute-by-minute, sometimes second-by-second, self-policing going on that nobody knew about, where I keep myself from blurting out what the HD inside is making me think. A cacophony of knee-jerk responses to words that might not be intentionally hurtful. I suppress them all. Explosions of rage against situations I cannot control. I sit on them all. I never take a break.

All of that builds up inside and there's so much pressure that it seeps out as a stopgap measure when I least expect it. When I least intend it or feel it. Say, in the morning when I'm having coffee and still finding my way out of the fog from the trazodone induced night of sleep before. Or when I'm trying to figure out some intangible issue and am asked about something in the here and now.

Times like that, when I'm not heavily, 100-percent self-monitoring, when I'm not fully clamped down on myself, it slips out without my control and creates the very effect I work all my waking hours to prevent. And it hurts people.

And when it happens, I'm either oblivious to what I'm doing because my attention is divided or I recognize the awful damage my geyser does when, in fact, I'm holding back my tsunami. My takeaways are that I cannot multitask attention and the need to forgive myself. More importantly, I can never, ever let the tsunami be released. I must be vigilant until my brain is damaged to the point that no medicine, philosophy or amount of willpower can stop it. Until the plates give way from the stress of it and the water rushes over to destroy everything I've built and every kind regard I've worked for.

Until then, it's important that the people in my life appreciate the Herculean effort that goes into my efforts to be normal. Throw in trigeminal neuralgia, colon motility issues and degenerative disc disease on top of that, and sprinkle with PTSD.

What is "cranky" for other people is, for me, a relative triumph, a relief. Catastrophe averted. For today.

Quiet seduction

Confusion about confusion, turning into itself again before leaving behind a raw, blistered, embarrassed, embarrassing, leftover me. Realizations these days are "Oh, it's happening," or, "My God, I can't stop it."

On the surface, I try to hide it or I pretend I don't know. That's easy enough when I stagger along. But when I try to talk and the words don't come out, I'm busted by fucking Huntington's disease. And there's no verbal conversation that I can have that isn't impaired. Unintelligible or a sick game of charades or both. It's so bad that I've found myself not saying things that I would normally say. I keep it all in the nonverbal realm. I keep it private. It feels safer and gives me more control.

I manage to croak out what I mean when pressured or if I'm left no choice. But it's easier just to let the world pass on by and keep the commentary to myself. Byproducts are that I am frequently misunderstood and my desires are not met. But that's on me. Nobody can read my mind.

Sometimes I stare at my husband and wish he knew what I was thinking, because it's too traumatic and laborious for me to try to verbalize it. When I do that, he often asks me what I'm thinking about and I'll pick an easier answer, like something we've just discussed or a familiar topic.

Oh, so that's why

I understand why they all became quiet. Quiet uncle. Quiet grandmother. Quiet mother who died a year ago this coming Monday. I'm beginning to understand what it cost them to enter into silence. I already understand why silence succeeded in seducing them.

Auditory memory woes

By the summer of 2018, it was taking a lot of energy to understand things. For a repeated sequence of events, I needed repeated verbal instructions. Case in point: That ziplining trip in the mountains when, after the initial training, I made sure I got the complete set of verbal instructions before every jump. Or when we got home from our mountain trip, the upstairs air conditioning wasn't working again. Randy had explained to me at least 30 times how it was supposed to work and what the problem was, but I keep cycling around to the question, "Why can't we just turn it all the way down and see if it works that way."

It bothered me that I couldn't understand.It bothered Randy because he thought he wasn't explaining it well enough or using the right tactic, but it wasn't his fault. I just couldn't retain the concepts as they related together, and every time I bore down and tried again I felt worse about my inadequacy. I felt like I was letting him down by not retaining the information.

I wanted to give up trying to understand this one. The repair people had been called. I could bang my head all day against a wall and get a better result than spending my time trying to understand the problem.It was just not in me anymore

– the capacity to grab a concept like that and hold onto it. I determined that I would stop myself after a few reps of explanations and ask myself if the knowledge being conveyed was critical. If not, I would opt to not understand it and be happier.

Randy has a wonderful sense of humor. When we met, I was able to give him a run for his money. I laughed a lot back then. I understood humor instinctively and responded reflexively. I've watched my perception of humor flatten and flatten and recede and recede day by day by day.

Waiting

It's not one of my strengths. HD has screwed up whatever wiring made waiting an activity I can cope with. It's sort of like the way I used to feel when I was really little and it was close to Christmas and I really, really wanted Christmas to be there, so badly it was even a little unpleasant. But I now just feel the unpleasant part, with an intensity as nagging and urgent as a bad urinary tract infection. The medicine I take is supposed to make waiting easier for me, but sometimes more and more things that I wait for to happen or to arrive pile up and it becomes harder to bear. Some things would bother anyone, like the boots I ordered from China that took four months to arrive.

But when I'm waiting for several things at the same time, I perseverate about them all, shifting back and forth between them. Checking my inbox for an overdue response, asking Randy to call service people to check the status of whatever order is pending – all benign actions, but HD causes me to fuel it with raw anxiety. My daydreams are about waiting for other, future happenings. Right now I can rattle off about 20 items on my unofficial wait list, a fact that disturbs me. By the end of the day, I'm weary of the hyper vigilance and totally disproportionate anguish I feel over waiting for mundane things to happen. After a certain point, only the optional extra sedative will take the edge off. It is no longer possible to watch TV or read or anything like that. Those activities are too challenging to help me unwind anymore. Sometimes, there's no unwinding from the waiting.

Chapter 18

The worst idea

Suicide is a very common route some people with HD take.

Sometimes, just trying to function day to day with HD, I screw up things around me so badly that the only way I can see to make the pain and shame of it stop (and this is new) is to honor it as a temporary condition and keep on living.

Taking my life is the worst idea in the world, I have realized. Unfortunately, it was the very first thought that screamed in my head when I found out I had HD. It has long whispering in the background during my own mental health challenges. I have an update call and action plan, so if I become dangerously impulsive, people can step in and help.

Apathy, which, if you want to pass the class, you must certainly identify as the Jedi Mind Fuck of Huntington's disease, came like a thief in the night and robbed me first of energy, then of confidence, and finally it muted my starting mechanism.

I'm encouraged by the fact that I can make small steps toward one of these larger goals and this develops a positive perseverance loop. I try to drown out the negative thoughts and replace them with working toward being the person I was because I now realize I genuinely liked her.

But apathy, T.J.M.F. of HD, rushes in like high tide at night a few mornings into my grand plan to reclaim some part of me, I wake up and can't remember or associate or connect myself with the conviction that I had. It's forever out of reach.

Again.

I've lost it for the millionth time. Multiply that disappointment by 3,650 nights. Then ask yourself how helpless you feel when someone who loves you so very much begs you to just try.

After failing to do things thousands of times, the voices that tell you to do them fade away and make way for the more basic, plaintive and private pleas – that you hope you can change your clothes or take a bath or brush your teeth this week.

That doesn't leave much else except the will to love and the will to live. I love people with all my heart. Once you're in, you're family unless you abuse my family.

After love, what is left is the will to live, which leads me back to the beginning of this entry. That first thought that has always been there in the din of thoughts, I've learned the hard way that it can be a dangerous loop to get caught up in.

Not too long before, I suffered an emotional upset, that left me feeling worthless and ashamed. My emotions quickly went out of my control, and I came too close to ending my life.

I'd been taking a medication as prescribed for several years. I figured I didn't really need it that much anymore. In my mind, it was so insignificant that my cessation of it wasn't worth mentioning to anyone. But, according to Dr. Vaishnavi, the effects of withdrawal combined with a growing propensity to act impulsively due to the chemistry of HD were major players in my suicide attempt.

I poured Tramadol and clonazepam on the bed. I texted my sons and husband goodbye, and started taking handfuls of pills. I immediately regretting taking the pills and was relieved when the EMTs got there. It was a very short ambulance ride to the ER. I slept there for 22 hours, I was committed to a psych ward in Winston-Salem and rode in the back of a deputy's car the whole way. I was shocked when I came to there because it was too bright. I couldn't believe where I was. When I awoke there, I attempted to resist checking in. I have snapshots of memories of resistance interspersed with comforting voices of nurses. I punched a wall in the hallway, I spoke mean gibberish when Randy called to check on me, which I remember none of. Then I was crying in the shower. I was checked on every seven minutes. I began going to groups and seeing doctors, I looked at my own behavior, I realized that I need to do the things I can do. I was checked on every fifteen minutes. It felt like an eternity waiting to be discharged and seeing Randy. The nurses were sincere and hugged me goodbye. The orderly took me out of the locked ward and to the elevator.

I saw Randy's face in the lobby. I was out of the hospital and into the sunshine. During the long ride home, we talked about the beginning of the pandemic.

I was forced to admit that I'm still worth something to someone.

The great equalizer

The COVID pandemic was a great equalizer in its own tragic way. Your life was now more like mine:

Your life was changed by a disease which can kill you. You were afraid for your own life and for the lives of your loved ones. You feared passing the disease to your family. You imagined the suffering you and they would endure and it made you anxious and depressed.

You had no way to stop it. No control.

Your livelihood had been affected.

You saw everything you do through the lens of the disease. You'd wake up and couldn't believe this was really happening. But it was. And you didn't cause it or ask for it. You felt alone.

But I no longer felt as alone in my experience because you all could relate now. To the fear. The dread. The helplessness. To the isolation.

Now we are alone together.

Hard to say as a state of mind

I woke up one morning to find that the connection between my body and mind, something I've always taken for granted, was inaccessible. I couldn't hold conversations. I couldn't take care of my own needs. I needed Randy's help for dressing and bathing. Everything that I have feared was happening without warning.

We determined that this was probably a transient adjustment and I'd get better. My neurologist explained that textbook Huntington's disease symptoms present gradually over time. You don't just wake up significantly worse. That's usually a sign of something else.

My psychiatrist told me that the degenerative brain process involves a lot of software workarounds. The brain's wiring faces an obstacle and sometimes there's a period where it has to figure out a workaround. It works around to function normally until it can't. Then the hardware itself starts to go.

The fact that I was able to articulate what was happening was evidence that a workaround was in progress, and I was encouraged to know that I have more time. Still, this experience gave me a glimpse into my future, and it was terrifying. The experience of being trapped within myself has always been something I dreaded.

But I came out of it with some measure of comfort.

Even though I couldn't communicate or take care of myself, I still loved. I still had feelings and ideas. But I also picked up on the devastation that my family endured. They lovingly met this lumplike version of me with incredible strength, concern, constructive optimism and creativity. They didn't set me aside because I didn't function. This rescued me from despair. Some days are going to be good days and some days will challenge us as a family. Some days will defy my worst expectations. I plan to seize the good days and enjoy them.

My manifestation manifesto

To understand what I have, it helps to know what I don't have.

I do not have a disease that grows tumors inside my body.

I do not have a disease that merely makes me move a lot, or be forgetful.

My disease will never go into remission or be reversible. My disease causes me to say and do things that ruin every holiday.

It manifests like an overloaded emotional pressure cooker. My disease contorts my personality and turns me into someone who hurts people to the point that they must withdraw to stay healthy themselves. Therapeutically detach. I know this about my disease. Everyone I love will endure emotional abuse caused if I have emotional issues that may not be controlled. That's what HD does. That's how it affected my mother, and her mother.

That's what it's doing to me.

No chemo, no pill, no radiation, no shots, no therapy can stop it. Not for lack of research. Research is being done, and my whole life I have heard that a cure is probably about five years away. In fact, in May 2025, a treatment is moving in the right direction.

In the meantime, we all live and pretend it isn't happening. We pretend that I am the same person I was at 18. At 21. At 35. I was born with a mutant gene that is now expressing itself by making me behave in ways I am ashamed of. I cry every day because of the person I can't stop becoming.

I mourn the loss of each me that I once was, and wish I had better appreciated each previous iteration of Sarah.

Instead, I squandered myself, worrying about how bad it would be. The losses already suffered and those to come. Now, it's showtime and not one of the millions of worries and bottles of beer that tainted my existence prepared me in any way to handle myself now.

I bring no skills to the table. No weapon.

The only comforting notion is that at least I can be assured that the person I am today is better, kinder, and more loving than the person I will be tomorrow.

Severe psychiatric symptoms description attempts

It becomes important that I describe my emotions in a way that make sense so the doctors would know what kind of drugs to prescribe: antipsychotics or mood stabilizers. Sometimes, severe psychiatric symptoms occur as part of the Huntington's disease life ruining extravaganza package.

One such experience was the emotional equivalent in intensity and horror to the pain I would feel if one of my eyelids had been pulled around my head, down to my neck, leaving behind my skinned, painful head, unable to see anything. Another way that could describe it is the emotional response someone had if their fingernails were being pulled out slowly, one by one, only worse.

This extreme negative arousal continued, and it manifested as my own screams and shrieks filling my head. I wanted to go through the house screaming and shrieking out loud, but I hid myself away from everyone else and it felt like my head was going to explode with the constant suppression of the screams of emotional pain.

The other part of this crisis was like a cloudy, smoky feeling of doom that washed in and swirled about while the first part was going on. It didn't use words, but it communicated to me that I couldn't handle much more of the first part, but warned that it may never stop. In fact, it could get worse and I could spend my life trapped in the first part with the second part swirling around. And that added more panic and hopelessness.

While in crisis, these two parts were incessantly occurring. But I noticed that it was quieter and easier to tolerate in the morning. It got louder and more painful and harder to bear throughout the day, until the evening when I'd run up to my bedroom, strap on the sleep apnea machine and take deep, deliberate breaths until I fell asleep.

These days, this type of episode has included, at least once that I know of, by psychosis. It turns out I was only dehydrated, but I thought my blood was evaporating, and that Randy wanted to kill me. It was scary and I take plenty of mood stabilizer to stay on top of that. Having read the above description the first time since my recent psychotic episode, it may be worth noting to someone, that the "cloudy, smoky" sinister feelings of doom was familiar, because it mimicked my psychotic voice.

Sometimes, no deep probing is required. Case in point: Keep hydrated!

Here's a little word sorbet to cleanse the palate:

I want to see my friends. I can't talk to any of them. I want to be alone.

There's none of me left. So even alone, I'm left with no one.

If a fleck of me flickers by, I'll grab it. And try to mold it into my game face before it dissipates.

Until then, I'll pile sleep upon itself. Folding away the danger of being understood.

Profundity and simplicity

When I was a young, active alcoholic, it was my obsession, whether I was drunk or not, to interpret the ordinary as the profound. This was an easy intellectual exercise for a drunk, and doing so made me the creator of endless epiphanies that, despite my frequent dissemination of them in the bars to anyone within earshot, were significant only to me.

A lot of my material came from advice I got from my dad when we drank scotch together. I hung on any words he uttered. Perhaps parts of what he said might have been profound. He was an intelligent, thoughtful man. But the things I fixated on were quite ordinary. A lot of the things he told me became my mantras during my drinking years.

Once, I went to him because I was having a great deal of trouble letting go of some emotional event and he said, quite seriously: "Erase it from your mind."

Ironically, whatever I shared with him that inspired him to say those words is collected in that ever-expanding universe that contains everything that is there from following his advice.

The alcoholic me latched onto the magical qualities in what he said. From now on, this was how I dealt with disappointments and kept traumatic events repressed. This, with a chaser, was how I ignored the possibility of HD being a part of me.

And some (one) discoveries are still amazing, like when I declared that the McDonald's pancake in the Cave parking lot was a portal to another world. So was early sobriety more than 30 years ago, I had to deal with some of the things that I had repressed. Life was very hard in early sobriety until I accepted that it was okay for my ideas to be ordinary and that they were, in fact, ordinary thoughts to begin with.

In fact I had learned to avoid magical thinking because, for example, it can justify taking a drink if you believe it. After several years passed and I learned that I have HD, when I was in a place of gratitude, I elevated the ordinariness of being able to function in any capacity to a higher level that, intellectually, I valued more than I used to. I could still hold down a job. I could maintain relationships. I could swallow food. I didn't wet the bed every night. Enlightened by HD, I viewed these activities as far more than mundane.

And the sublime?

One day I listened to Itzhak Perlman play the "Theme from Schindler's List" and my spirit remained transfixed in this elevated place until I forgot that I'd heard it. Could having HD make such enormous beauty more impossible *not* to succumb to, or does it flatten everything, as I thought?

Anyway, my dad ended up having a stroke that decimated his short-term memory. We were forced to have the same, simple conversation every five minutes for what I thought was too many years. Kidney failure finally claimed my father and, I later learned, the toxicity of that disease makes people say strange things.

Four years prior, I'd stood at the foot of his death bed. I was still struggling with my diagnosis and I was losing my dad. Some of the final words he said were directed at me. He said: "Be sad or be glad." Given our history, and given my history, how could I not make this my mantra? It's a simple choice that I remind myself I have when I sense that HD is overshadowing everything. And I will always regard his words as quite profound.

Upon reflection, this can be my psychiatric equation for success.

My mother ended

On December 6, 2016, my mother's earthly existence ended. I have said that I lost her to HD years and years ago, but she and everyone close to her were victims of her primary behavior symptom: the ever-renewing anger loop. Only during the past couple of years did she take any medicine for HD. She refused until, somehow, doctors convinced her that she would feel better if she took medicine to slow her chorea, and when she started taking that medicine a lot of the anger went away. Her anger, no, that is unfair to her: the anger. I've spent years in therapy dealing with the hell that she put me through before I knew she had HD and started realizing that the problem wasn't me. I've spent those same years trying to forgive her for hurting my family and other people I love because her behavior was caused by a disease. Our disease. Now, just my disease. I have Facebook friends who've lost their moms to HD and they love and miss those moms. I wished that my mom was like theirs. I felt that way about my dad, who was never abusive. I grieved when he died and the empty spot that he used to fill, I carry still. But with my mom, first disbelief that her dynasty of terror had ended. Part of me never expected it to happen. Then, all I could feel was relief. There was no longer a microcosm of hurt and bruised energy swirling around her demands or reacting to her use of the most hateful words she could spit out. For her memorial service, we put together a presentation of the good in her, before the disease changed her. We had to go far back. I hoped that being reminded that she was a healthy, kind person once, a person who did nice things, would help me in the forgiveness department. Even more, I wanted to be happy for her. Happy that she was free from the disease. Happy that she was no longer out of control. Happy that she was at peace. But on the day after she died, someone asked me how I was feeling, and before I could think of what I was supposed to say, I replied, "Fuller." And in that moment, it was true. The days following my mom's death tumbled on top of each other. I never was able to visit her as much as she wanted me to. Even when I visited her every day, she would barely let me out the door. Even when she was yelling at me, she didn't want me to go. She wanted the connection. I moved away, my own HD progressed and I became less capable of making the 90-minute drive. Then she started calling me, literally hundreds of times a day. She would sit for hours and hit the redial button and when I'd answer she'd ask me when I was coming to visit. When my support system got wind of this, they insisted that I block her calls so I could try to get something done during the day and not have my heart broken every time I heard the despair in her voice and felt the specter of what could befall me. I told her I was having trouble with my phone. She mailed me a few letters begging me to help her, but I confirmed that she was safe and being well taken care of. The letters stopped and I visited

141

as often as I could. At a certain point, long before her final days, she'd decided that she wanted to consume me. I don't know if it was the same dynamic as the time I was drowning and as people kept trying to save me I climbed up their bodies, plunging them farther down into the water. But for years I've felt her sickness manifested in a need for something from me that I could neither identify nor satisfy. Until she died, I carried an enormous weight of guilt because I thought that I wasn't there enough for her. That I couldn't see her or help her. That I had failed the one who had failed me the most, and that by doing so I'd blown both of our chances for redemption. Now even though she was gone, I still had a sense of her being. The memory of her unforgettable presence lingered and, more and more, I remember snapshots in my life from the times long ago when she showed me love. But the oppressive guilt lifted. I realized that I did the best I could, based on my own condition. And I felt relief knowing she was released from her diseased body and mind and no longer desperate. Now it was my turn to live out my days. I needed to make adjustments to improve my health. I formulated safeguards to protect my kids from what I went through. I began having conversations with them about blocking me if I perseverate on the phone. And I conveyed my unconditional love to them the best I could.

Let the show begin

The real onset has kicked in, and it doesn't feel very slow. It feels like I'm being pulled in by the undertow over and over. Miles out. Into a dry

ocean.

My thoughts are duller and they no longer fall over each other. There's starting to be space between them.

I'm unintentionally oblivious toward daily life. I've stopped cooking. I seldom use the car. I've stopped engaging with others unless I'm directed or scheduled to. I know there's a lot of home improvement that I want to happen, but either it can't happen soon enough or I don't have faith it will happen at all.

The emotions I feel the most are impatience with myself for not being able to do anything right and regret when I hurt people. The collection of memories and facts I've forgotten has outgrown its habitat. It needs an island of its own.

I sound like I'm drunk and people on the phone who don't know me are put off by it. My brain feels thickened with obstacles, too sick with HD, to be written about with any great insight by its owner.

My experience of cognitive losses were disturbing. I was a remnant of a cork bobbing up every now and then in a turbulent, empty ocean.

Meanness lite

My anger always tastes bitter and I tried to keep it in but I say something mean. Then it was too late and I'd ruined something. A reputation, a conversation, a relationship, an evening. A family. The thing that made me angry and then mean was gone, but I was left alone with my meanness. Nobody wants to be around someone who's mean, not even me.

But I couldn't get away from myself. I was lonely and I wanted to be around other people, but I was afraid of what I'd do to them. If this time would be the time that I went too far. That I broke a heart or burned a bridge too completely.

Being mean was the part I'd feared the most. They told me that lots of people with HD aren't mean. They told me that just because my mother was mean didn't doom me to meanness.

They told me that my true, kind nature would be exaggerated. They were wrong. And now I was mad at them too because I bought into their wishful thinking.

Every time it happened, it was harder to bounce back. Every time it happened, I felt less of myself left. I thought back to when I was 20-something and I laughed and jumped from rooftop to rooftop with my friends in our platform shoes. That girl could never come back, and I missed her.

Falling

May is HD Awareness Month and my awareness of my own HD increased greatly when I fell on my ass one May Friday night. I was allowing myself to be dragged to a play and just one more time I had wanted to wear shoes with a little lift. But right after putting them on, I tried to walk backwards in them and that set off a slow motion, reverse fall to the ground.I went to the play, but was too sore by intermission to stay. It pretty much ruined everyone's weekend because I was laid up with a bruised hip and not happy.

When I fell, my self-perception landed outside of me, like a camera, giving me snapshots of where I was now. The trauma of the fall spawned a temporary worsening of everything.

Besides poor balance, I couldn't remember life events. There were chunks of my life that just weren't there and I didn't know it until someone mentioned it.

I now had trouble doing simple things like making phone calls. I had unrealistic ideas and I expected things around me to be the way they always had been, but they couldn't be, because I needed the environment to be adapted for my altered condition. I didn't act the same way. The most insignificant things, like making simple choices, were huge, emotional deals that were liable to piss me off or leave me with hot tears of frustration.

Even thinking of reaching out to friends felt like running underwater, so I stopped before I reached. I was afraid I wouldn't reach them, and if I did reach them what was left of me to connect with?

I now felt like the memories I had were from someone who existed two personalities ago. That the changes in who I am were stark and permanent.

After the falling-on-my-ass incident, I felt overwhelmed by the notion that my family needed respite. That I'd pushed everyone to the edge. They told me no, today is a new day and things are okay, and I tried hard to let that sink in. But with HD, the promise of a new day brought with it the promise that I was slipping, I was falling. And worst of all, I was becoming a stranger.

Chapter 19

Reassignment of everything

The same amount of energy I once used to mourn my original personality, instead allows me to concentrate on chewing soft food, on each swallow, and on waiting until my mouth is empty to speak. The energy I allotted to tending my zoo of pet neuroses is nearly enough to brush and pet the stalwart Rupee.

My efforts to do things or make things right succeeded on any level is now put to use trying to figure out what that could be...

The shock never goes away.

Or wondering if the love I've tried to express was received as coming from the me of today, or a haunted, unreachable and possibly cruel stranger who we all see me becoming will replace me and linger for years to come?

Throughout this book, (as in the previous paragraph) I have noticed that I have been perseverating on the angst. It must be self-soothing, in that I know what my present feelings feel but don't know about the ones to come. I want to react a different way.

Becky Gaeta relieved me years ago of the responsibility of being in charge what other people think or do. That means I let go of wondering what, if any, impression I have made on the world. I can let go of wondering whether a flicker of the wisdom that is supposed to come with age survived in the wake of HD's wakening.

Randy and I realize that this is not another blip, but is indeed the clinical version of onset. I told him I was scared and he looked at me with his beautiful blue eyes that I fell in love with so long ago and said, "You have every right to be afraid."

His words gave me strength for a lot of reasons. It reaffirmed what I have always known, that he is going to be real with me as the shit begins to hit the fan. And I needed that. I needed to introduce myself to the condition of physical decline and deal with it the same way I had dealt with the weight gain, trigeminal neuralgia, depression, anxiety, paranoia, irritability, difficulty focusing, trouble sleeping and so on.

Research the hell out of it, talk to other doctors and other people about it, and work with Randy to make a plan.

And then live by that plan.

Part of that plan for me is losing the word "horrible." I banish it from my typing for a few years and now I feel it nosing its way in.

If I could allow myself limited use to describe why it is not necessary, "horrible" was linked with the emotion fear, which I am kicking to the curb as well.

Our children are now adults. At this moment, everybody seems to be pursuing their dreams without hindrance, which is my dream come true for them.

Since we moved to Western N.C., we don't visit each other that much, but we feel their love.

Apologies to Randy, whose grandfather literally did step in front of a train, but I would (metaphorically) jump in front of a locomotive if it provided our family a cure. There's much hope in that department, and I think that hope and fear can note thrive within the same state of mind.

I write this trying not to enter a frenzied state as each day it becomes harder to type.

I type, accidentally delete, undo, repeat.

Still, I can get some mileage out of the notion that, until now, I have excelled at explaining things I can no longer do.

Like Charlie in "Flowers for Algernon," by Daniel Keyes, I am aware of and pained by every regression, every loss of knowledge, every weakening.

Looking back and moving forward

We learned that my grandmother had HD late in her life. Before then, when I was young, I spent the night at her house a lot and, from a child's point of view, the disease manifested in two ways: she ate funny and it took her an eternity to walk.

I noticed the walking especially at night. She began her trip to the bathroom while I was still awake. I would hear a familiar, irregular patting of her feet touching the floor. When I first heard her foot hit the floor, I pretended I was asleep but was really watching to see how long it took her to get to the bathroom. There were periods where she was still. Then she would make a few hurried steps, then wait a long time for the next step to come. The steps went sideways, backwards, forwards and diagonal. When she was about to pass by my bed, I held my breath for as long as I could so she wouldn't know I was awake.

Sometimes I thought my cheeks would pop open, but she

never caught me watching her. I'll bet I watched her walk to that bathroom at least a hundred times when I was little. It was fascinating to me that she could move that way. I didn't associate it with anything bad, or sick or wrong. That was just how Baboo got from one place to another.

Fast-forward 45 years and my grandmother had been dead for 21 of them. But I hadn't forgotten how she wore her hair in plaits pinned in a bun with hairpins. I hadn't forgotten that she made biscuits using lard and wrung the necks of chickens.

And I especially hadn't forgotten how she moved. More and more, my own body reminded me of hers as it struggled to somehow approximate and perfect the gait she created. Especially at night and especially going to the bathroom. I looked down at the dark floor and let the steps fall where they may, my hands outstretched. Each night, for a moment, in my sleepiness, I imagined that I was her, with the stops and starts and eternal, bizarre march.

But I wore my hair long and loose. I made scones with real butter, but often mistake sugar for salt. I couldn't touch a dead, raw chicken, much less kill one. By the time I made it to the bathroom, my surroundings reminded me that it was me in the bathroom. Me with HD. And soon I began the slow marathon back to bed, glad no one is watching

I'm pretty sure my precious Baboo and Aunt Naomi were thinking about all sorts of things as one stood like a statue, still and silent, and the other, like a parrot with minimal talent, could only ask how people were.

I saw my uncle H.W.'s contentment, when we began to spring him from confinement, sitting in my living room while Mortimer, my pet starling, who, unlike my aunt, had an enormous vocabulary, landed on his head. Now its my turn to become the person that people ask, without ill intent, how I am doing as if I wasn't in the room.

"Does she understand?"

"What can I expect?"

"She is a different person."

"She is a shell." Wait a minute.

I am no fucking shell.

I will never be a shell.

I will be unable to communicate, have poor judgment, and have limited ability to regulate body functions. I won't be able to process what I hear, decide on my answer, and put my answer into words or code or even scribbles.

Even I bought into that shell notion for a while.

But I was insulting my future self by calling her a husk.

A monster.

A mutant.

Being propelled further into the later stages of HD, I see that thinking of my ancestors as shells of their former selves was a cop out.

An excuse to not visit them. They wouldn't remember anyway. But they did.

Huntington's disease naturally lends itself to being misunderstood. Being recast as a person, patient, partner, parent and friend.

My Uncle H.W. was kept in a nursing home on paralytic sedation that we were told was for his safety. He was taken off that medication, and Joe Warren, his best friend, visited. H.W. jumped out of bed and revealed that he was still Dub.

He hopped in Joe's car and enjoyed being driven around.

Dub was capable when someone thought he was himself and expected him to do things.

When he couldn't walk or talk, he yelled expletives at the caregivers, and, in return, they medically managed him.

What if that's me in 5-7 years? Can I come up with a life hack or so for not repeating that sort of ending?

We were with him and watched him take his last breath, and were relieved that his decades-long fight was over. He was exhausted.

I hope that having splayed my family's journeys here can lead anyone who wonders, to a greater understanding of my family's experience as different forms of human beings.

Genetically mutilated

The descent into contamination when finding out I have always had the mutated gene.

The grappling with a seemingly endless engorgement of guilt.

I think, based on the way things have been, I will continue to lose the skill of describing how my body reacts to the onset of the disease.

That inescapable, maddening conundrum of becoming symptomatic while becoming unable to describe it:

That's the reason for this book.

I speak for my grandmother, who deserves to be known by her beautiful name, Eva Kate. I speak for my Aunt Naomi, whom young me shouldn't have laughed about. I speak for my Uncle H.W. I speak for my mother, who did the best she could helping three HD patients while enduring it herself.

I'm in pursuit of the very moment I can neither write nor talk nor move.

I intend to run so fast that I stop the passage of time, long enough to stand in front of these dreaded milestones and say,

"Don't give up on me. Don't leave me behind. Because I am

still here."

My dementia – and I only call it that because you will not understand it if I say my dark foreboding brain disintegration – is taking away another layer of me.

I learn workarounds until there are no more workarounds.

Until it is metal scraping metal.

Until it is jagged glass crumbling in on itself.

Until I have lost control like one of those bloated dead hogs that floats by after its environment drowns it. After a flood it can't escape.

I feel irretrievably lost when I tangle with this host of conditions: Fucking it up, forgetting how to do it, and hurting other people.

Some days, they vie to replace every crumb of my personality.

Every drop of my goodness.

Every spark of hope in my heart.

You can't understand what I am saying or mean to say.

Sleep is hard to come by.

I'm too scared to take the stairs out front or out back.

Pills feel lodged in my throat.

I eat soft food and it goes down the wrong way.

I'm being run over by the train I have long feared, long heard in the distance.

I have childish desires and emotions.

I chase shiny things to avoid fixating on what's happening to me. Therein lies a tool I may need now: the shiny.

My mother in law, who Mark called Grandma Jewelry instead of Julie, was drawn to shiny and sparkly items. I imagine that it kept her mind busy and gave her a good stream of dopamine.

While I am in declaring mode, hear this: I'm finished feeling guilty for not wanting to do things.

It's what the disease is telling me to do. Sitting in my house looking out the window is no tragedy for me. I am quite comfortable and it keeps me safer than messing around in the kitchen where only yesterday I microwaved a jar of peanut butter with metal in it.

The best I can do is good enough. Each day, the best I can do shrinks but gone is the need to apologize for it. There's really no reason to hold on to any bitterness born from comparison. There never was.

I excise my shame from Huntington's disease. My ancestors and I are not morally flawed.

I'm letting go of the perception that HD's stigma is equal in intensity to that of a sexual offender.

I am letting me be the me I am becoming and giving that new Sarah a break. Perhaps I can apply some Newcomers club activities for her.

My short term destination is beyond all of the fear, disappointment, and heartbreak.

It's where good days are possible.

Tradition and apathy

When we lived in New Bern, I went from being able to decorate a tree to not being able to. I couldn't break it all down into tasks and initiate them.

My friend, Ari, came over the last few years and decorated it for me. She would give me directions and I would follow them. Those were some trees.

I feel unconditional positive regard for people who I am friends with. Forever and ever. Many of those friends have cut their losses with me over the years, starting as early as I can remember.

Those who rescue the discarded me eventually feel their lives derailed by my train wreck of a disease. They bail or they fade silently into the background, mistaking the latter approach to be the humane one. What is left of my brain thinks that people are entitled to the lives they want.

But dementia and perseveration lead me to dwell on the bad decisions I have made. After a certain point, sorry didn't make things go away anymore.

How it goes

I dropped a piece of tissue and picked it up off the floor and it fell out of my hand. I picked it back up and it fell out again and again and again. I leaned forward to grab it tightly and I knocked over the trash can. I staggered trying to refill the trash can because I was dropping and dropping. I left the bathroom and nobody saw it.

But it really happened. It's happening. A kajillion times a day. I'm in danger of cracking glasses and plates that just want to be cleaned and put away with no molestation. I fill out a form and it feels like I'm using the pen for the first time.

I'm no longer connected to the movements it makes. I sit on the couch and wait. Wait until I am unable to go have lunch or shop for clothes or go for a drive or hang out with the boys. Those are the only things that are not noticeably muted, emotionally and physically draining, or completely daunting. I am really able to brush my teeth and shower but it's so hard to do that, it's painful and I give up doing it. The same way I gave up on algebra. I can still take a walk but going outside tends to turn my skin and my soul inside out.

If I get beyond the pain of the quick ripping off, those things actually help me.

To walk and to brush and to shower.

But afterwards it hurts. Like being out in the sun too long. Like wallowing in acid rain.

And it takes days to heal, but never quite heals all the way. So every time, to avoid that old familiar discomfort, I want to try a little less.

Chapter 20

Conversion

One Monday morning, I woke up, got out of bed and couldn't walk well at all. I'd been having balance issues for a while but was walking fine. What began happening that morning wasn't a stagger or a stumble or anything I'd ever envisioned I would do or had seen my relatives do. I shuffled. A Parkinson's-like shuffle.

Hard to put one foot in front of the other. Small steps. Not covering much ground.

Two neurologists told me that it couldn't be HD. It came on too suddenly and had the wrong movement MO. I should investigate other areas. And I knew nothing about other areas.

Over the next week, I learned about drug-induced Parkinson's symptoms. I learned about Lewy bodies, just enough to scare me.

Each day since it started had gotten worse. My doctor ordered me a wheelchair. Randy had to line one up to borrow so he could push me around if we had to go out before insurance approved my order.

But by the time he'd made that arrangement, my walking had

deteriorated to the point that it was just alternating sets of toe clawing. Nothing else happened. He called to see if he could borrow instead a chair I could push myself around the house in. I had to use a makeshift bedpan at night.

Randy began rearranging furniture to make the house wheelchair accessible. We were both silently hoping we could get a chair narrow enough to roll through the old bathroom door. We were hoping for the best, but planning for the worst. I wondered if I'd walked my last step. Was this going to work its way up my body and immobilize it all? Was it going to have its own accompanying horror show of symptoms for me to dread, or would it take me out so fast I wouldn't have time to go there? Randy and I were on our own in uncharted territory.

Over the next few days, my brain told my legs to move, but they didn't act on the message. That's what the doctors said. The jury was still out over whether it was due to HD or my brain's response to some upset. The only way I'd know was if I got better. Usually people with HD who have apraxia have it in their arms instead of their legs. In fact, in my limited research, I'd found no documentation on apraxia and walking and HD.

Randy and I went to Duke University Medical Center, in Durham, two hours from our home. We returned home with a long running set of appointments with a physical therapist who was going to teach me how to walk again. And they did.

The memory of those weeks hung fresh like some freaky nightmare. The joy I felt when I took, at age 51, those new first steps, the happiness I felt, the desire to never again sit down or lie down or turn down any invitation to go for a walk again – that's something I hope I'll remember forever.

Peace

Randy noticed it first. When I learned to walk again, my stride was longer than it had ever been before. Before I forgot how to walk, I trailed behind him when we were out on out walks. Now he could barely keep up with me.

Improvement had pervaded many other aspects of my life. I was exuberant, capable and joyfully doing things I previously was unable to do, like grocery shop and cook dinners. Eager for errands and outings, I now said yes instead of no. I was present in the moment and I sparkled.

I didn't know what has happening to me, but it seemed as likely as anything else that my brain had sort of a hard restart and my abilities got reset to a previous, more gloriously normal level of functionality. And I was grateful for all of it. It was worth the time in the wheelchair, the ensuing medical bills, if this was what came of it.

My lesson: You just never know why things happen.

Sometimes, like then, I catch a glimpse of a divine reordering. I'm standing under the flow of life and transmuting energy into joyful, grateful existence. I'm embodying the energy that was returned to me, and going with it.

I was now saying yes to walks in the neighborhood, to bicycle rides, to going to the pool at the Y. Every time I said yes, I felt liberated. Every time I did the activity I'd agreed to, I felt happy.

I was grateful.

I've been strapped into the seat of a carnival ride, whisking me through my beautiful life. I've put my hands in the air and been carried fearlessly throughout recent events. So much beauty to appreciate. So much love to reciprocate, including being there for people I love when they've needed me.

I'm grateful for the strength. For the newfound ability to cry "Yes!" And for the will to be my own agent in hard times and use the resources that are there for me. My will to make the right choices is my superpower. My love for my family and friends is infinite. I'm staying on this ride.

Peace in the totality

On August 21, 2017, I saw the total eclipse of the sun. Conditions were perfect in the mountains of Western North Carolina. Randy and Mark were there. During the moments before and after the period of totality, Noah and Ezra contacted me, so I was sharing the experience with people I was connected to by blood and by love.

The time before and after the totality evoked a different feeling than the totality did. Before and after felt like I was participating in a cool science experiment. But the moment the moon completely blocked out the sun, things changed. Crickets chirped. A strange semi-darkness prevailed. Bats came out. And I took off the eclipse glasses and looked up at a black orb proudly displaying its blackness in contrast with the white corona that surrounded it. It was like a secret planet had revealed itself. We all felt primal and slightly hallucinogenic. There was nothing to do but transfix my gaze at the totality.

To drink in the sight of it.

There was no Huntington's disease to consider for two minutes and 34 seconds. I was part of the human tribe. Energized. Feeling both very small and very large.

Directions to and from psychiatric challenges

First there's a bad place and then, there's the way to get there.

Cogitating from among negative, unpleasant or questionable ideas can send me downhill quickly. My brain begins to disagree with itself, and that's reflected in the following thought patterns: an inner scream, an inner argument and an inner struggle to stop the screaming and arguing. Periodically, my brain will seize on an incorrect or extraneous circumstance and unsuccessfully try to channel some of the brain screaming there.

I wonder if this is what it was like for Mama?

Perhaps, I thought, there was no place where these rogue thoughts belonged and that's why they stuck around. So around and around I went, barely keeping it together. Saved only by routine.

When people scratched my surface, they were far away. At first, I couldn't understand what their words meant. What their intentions were. If I'd done something wrong. My brain revved up with even more interference and I might smile at them and feel so distant from them and wondered if they pitied me yet.

By the end of each day, I was more tired than the day before.

At the end of each day, when I did a mental inventory of my faculties, they seemed smashed and bruised.

At the end of the day, I was so worn out with struggling with myself that I just wanted the day to end like flicking off a light.

But my body kept me awake, flicking and twitching, like some roll call of inventory of parts that malfunctioned. Once I put a thumb under each side of my butt to keep my arms still at night. My right thumb was sore and sprained.

Postcard from a panic attack

It has been years since I have had one. I think its because my stress level is much lower and I catch anxiety early and use medication to stabilize. This is a recap of a doozy a few years ago:

I found myself wrapped inside rhythmic panting. Each breath

was chained to a mournful, fearful and painful cry. A scream. My body is raping me emotionally. Caged by fear, my senses are limited to hearing the muffled sounds that permeate the din of my screams.

My eyes won't work. My words won't come.

Alone seemingly forever, but suddenly my 14-year-old son's arms surround me.

"Mom, what's wrong. What can I do?"

I want to tell him to stay but my words are trapped by my mantra. He holds me and I thank God. It goes on for longer than it ever has. Longer than it ever should. No words can get out. Thank God, I hear my husband on the stairs and then feel his presence in the room and my reassurance builds enough that my mouth sputters:

"pills, pills, pills, pills ..."

He brings them. The screaming slows to heavy breathing, then gives way again to weeping. I fall into myself a little bit as they help me from my office chair to my bed. Still catatonic from the emotional experience. Having slow uncertainties about how it will unravel.

I lay as if paralyzed on my side. "vomit vomit vomit vomit."

I say it until someone comes in the room. Are you alright? Are you going to vomit? They figure it out and a basin appears by my mouth.

"hot hot hot hot hot"

I say it and start to cry until they figure it out and I am undressed. "ice ice ice ice"

Until ice cubes are by my mouth where I can lick them. More meds come, and I make a trip to the bathroom. Normalcy approaches. The view from my tomb was my family who I felt and knew were there even when I couldn't tell them.

Crossed signals and full bladders

The emotional and the physical intertwine in a new way to help me recognize my body's signals. Sometimes I can't detect my body's signals telling me that there's a problem. My emotions go on high alert instead to let me know that something was wrong.

There was a learning curve in noticing emotional changes as signals of physical conditions. Remembering to look at emotional responses has paid off every time and spared me from a lot of anguish. Still, it was like learning a new language.

Here's an example. Sitting on my porch has always been satisfying. One day, I was irritated by a car that simply drove by. I wondered if this was the way my life was going to be from then on. That notion sent my brain further into turmoil. A pattern was noticed: edgy, then upset, then so upset I had to stop what I was doing so I could keep it together. I could think of no emotional cause or stimuli to make me upset. So, what was different?

I was undergoing physical therapy because of disc issues in my neck, up where it meets my head.

With the memory, the physical pain surfaced. Vague at first. Then it would join together with the emotional upset and change the emotional pain to turbo charged physical pain.

For some reason, I couldn't feel it physically, so I mistook the disturbance as emotional pain. Due to my memory issues, I'd been forgetting it was transpiring because nobody else was there when it happened.

I used to have severe panic attacks 30 minutes away from home after driving most of the back from my parents' house.

It started on the same stretch of Highway 70 coming back from Kinston. I put Randy on speakerphone when I got near that stretch so he could talk to me until I got home.

We spent time in therapy and at home trying to figure out why it was happening. Then Randy realized that the first thing I did when I got home was run to the bathroom and urinate. The anxiety attacks were because of a full bladder. I simply had to pee.

A pit stop in the middle of my return trips put an end to the full bladder and stopped the anxiety attacks that I feared would prevent me from driving.

Mother's day should be an extra Father's day around here

Randy,

On Mother's Day I decided that I would write this to you on Father's Day. Who knew that this weekend would be a challenge? Who knew that my healthy streak would threaten to end, shaking me and thereby shaking you?

I know it doesn't feel that way right now, but you're the person who is loved by all of us just for being you. You're the most important thing to us. And you ARE funny even though I can't laugh. I still know you're funny and I appreciate it for the sake of those who can laugh. You've tried and tried to break through to me until you're worn out.

I can't deny that I wish I didn't bring the HD to the table. But I've told myself that I'm only going to allow myself to feel like a victim one day a year. And it ain't today. Therefore, I suck it up and look for the silver lining:

Maybe the best Father's Day gift, besides the camera you're going to pick out, is for you to rest and take care of yourself. Mark and I love you more than anything and we want you to have peace.

Always, Sarah

Chapter 21

Present conditions

We moved to the mountains from our home of New Bern in 2021 because I perseverated about it, looked at a billion houses, and packed up everything except Randy's good ladder. Being surrounded by mountains has made me realize that I don't have to be entertained every moment. I watch a lot of TV because I have forgotten even the basic gist of every book I ever read. I stream music and make playlists to send to the boys. I don't have to be five minutes from the hospital.

I am lucky that my progression is slower than other people's and that HD is hitting me later in life than it could. I pray for everyone else who is suffering worse than I am. The people who got tested today. The people who got their results today. The people who lost their loved ones today.

Everything is getting worse at the same time, some things gradually, like swallowing and some things not, like impulse control. I'm short-circuiting. It's harder to find the words when I'm writing. I'm starting to spell words funny. Some days, I feel a big change coming on that I can't describe.

Around January 2024, I stopped taking a mood stabilizer, and my wanting of things, of making deals for houses and cars, just ceased. The urge to overeat finally let go as well.

But there was movement in its stead. First, it was only when I was really tired. Then, it was only when I came home from an outing because I attempted to be still and it took a lot out of me. I am wobbly and wiggly with poor balance and screwed up reflexes. I jiggle, especially when I try not to jiggle.

By January 2025, movement is nonstop, and I accidentally break dishes and glasses by banging them on the sink or counter. We use unbreakable things now. Sometimes I twist a knee when standing up or a knee adds an extra measure of effort that hurts or threatens my balance. My muscles clench up tightly and remain clenched for days. I like to call it "permaclench." No bath, medication or exercise helps. At night sometimes, my legs just flail. It reminds me of when my mom cooked frog legs and they jumped on the cast iron skillet. And speaking of cooking: When I try to cook, I burn pans, food and my skin.

Swallowing has become difficult, but I got my esophagus stretched for the second time next month and it helps. Aspiration pneumonia is the second largest cause of death for people with HD.

Suicide is the first.

Cardiac arrhythmia took my beloved Baboo away, so I recently wore a cardiac monitor to establish the baseline. Dealing with all of these malfunctions requires time and organization and the ability to multitask and problem solve. I've tried and failed a few times to bring on board a conductor of sorts to be in charge of my care. It's not covered by health plans that I have access to.

The pressure of setting all of these things in motion at once felt overwhelming. Fortunately, when I had a swallow study done, I met Sandra Hogsed, the speech therapist at Murphy Medical Center, which is a 30-minute drive from my home. In mountain miles, that's practically next door.

Duke Center of Excellence has, for years, encouraged me to participate in physical therapy, occupational therapy and speech therapy. Before I was symptomatic, I refused to attend therapy. At some point, I was told the reason I wasn't doing things was because I wasn't motivated. I rejected semantically the motivation reasoning because, to me, it tacitly implies fault, and I have reached my lifetime quota for self-abuse.

I am more like a brand-new riding mower with no starter. Sometimes, I'm a rocket stuck on many launchpads. I've spent days, weeks and years sitting on the couch doing nothing all day because I couldn't get started. When you don't get started, in my experience becomes harder and harder to get started.

Sandra Hogsed arranged for me to have speech therapy with her, then OT and PT, at the neighborhood hospital rehabilitation center. I went through a course of sessions that ran back to back to back a couple of times a week. The therapists are friendly, positive and serious about helping me. I feel understood there. They embolden me with creative ways to support living independently. I can't wait to resume, in fact.

I have a service dog, a yellow Labrador Retriever named Rupee. He was trained by prison inmates during the pandemic. Eyes Ears Nose and Paws is the company that matched us and a rigorous training program taught me how to be his partner. Rupee helps me walk, pick up things, open and close doors and get help. When my brain goes haywire, he's there before I know it, and lies on me like a 65-pound weighted blanket. Right now, he is laying on my foot and its keeping it from twitching.

He's an important member of the family. He is named after the currency but really named after my dear friend Paul Price's dog, who, unlike Paul, lived to be ancient.

Insatiable appetite for awareness

Anyone who has watched a person they love be taken by HD, peck by peck, knows that this hunger for heightened awareness is insatiable.

About 10 years ago, on the heels of the ALS ice bucket challenge, I launched a Pie in the Face for Huntington's disease campaign to raise awareness.

People with HD, researchers and politicians up for reelection participated. The videos brought a few seconds of joy and silliness. That was a great gift, and I should have left it at that. Instead, I got mad when people didn't understand HD well enough to raise awareness. We failed to reach enough people outside of the HD community bubble to help spread the word. I am open to any efforts to raise awareness, including receiving more pies on my face. My freezer will never not have Cool Whip.

The variety and severity of symptoms of HD and JHD lead to a conundrum or two. Simply stated, we people who have HD and our caregivers have all we can handle and may be too burned out to raise awareness for our own plight.

With my self-styled efforts to raise awareness, have felt as if I were beating my head against a wall.

But the wall I was beating my head against was created by me.

While anger is a symptom of HD, it's not a great tool to build anything, including awareness.

On the other hand, maybe folks don't think HD is worth having a cultural dialogue about because our ignored and potentially enraged community isn't jumping up and down.

I have seen the movie, "Complete Unknown" that steps right over Woody Guthrie's Huntington's disease diagnosis.

I thought that was a missed opportunity to raise awareness, and I reached out to one of the film's producers, brought the missed opportunity to his attention, and moved on spiritually. Maybe the Guthrie family have combat fatigue themselves.

Everyone has different caps on how much interfacing with the world they can do.

It's a blessing for the collective spirit of popular culture that nobody really famous currently has Huntington's disease. The obscurity of the disease creates a disconnect that has yet to be bridged.

One of my stepsons, Cole, now an adult with a rich sense of humor, played T-ball as a lad, and at the end of the year, he got a trophy. "Well," he said, "I finished that sport!" He never played baseball again because, in his mind, he had already done it.

A think that a similar pattern stunts effort to raise awareness of HD. If someone has done one thing, they honestly believe they have done enough, or at least done their part. They got the trophy. Or they took the pie. Or they made the donation.

Now they can run like hell to the next cause.

I wrote an article for the *Cherokee Scout* in Murphy, NC, in February 2025 that describes the generational nature and my family's experience with HD. The publisher, David Brown, was kind and stated that he hoped that the article had reached whomever I wanted to reach. And I have been thinking about that since February.

Who do I want to reach? Aside from a treatment or cure, what is enough?

- Enough would be cable news health channels having specials that featured families with Juvenile Huntington's disease and Huntington's disease.
- Enough would be knowledge of and support of agencies that support HD families, like HD Reach and Help4HD and the duplication of these agencies.
- Enough would be having a Jerry Lewis telethon for 500 years.
- Enough would be a Marlo Thomas commercial for a JHD Research hospital.
- Enough would be round-the-clock news cycles for HD breakthroughs.
- Enough would be the cast and viewership of Virgin River knowing as much about HD and JHD as they know about breast cancer.
- Enough would be the public's consumption of books, songs, creations about HD.
- Enough would be church and health department programs to help struggling HD and JHD families subsist.
- Enough would be Bob Dylan and his family being outspoken advocates for HD families.
- Enough would be many specialized hospitals for HD and JHD.
- Enough would involve being seen without prejudice.
- Enough would be a seat at the table, an invitation to the party.
- Enough would feel like being recognized.

David, I think that's a reasonable and humane ask.

My realizations collect in real time

As we hurtle to the end of this memoir, here's what I am facing and what I have learned. My lack of luck and financial savvy I group together in the same schemata as my cognitive challenges and try to accept it all in one clump.

One day I woke up and realized that those postponed grand adventures would not occur. Parenthood and being Randy's partner are primally satisfying. But what to do about the expectations of younger me, the me who knew that I wouldn't have HD, or that it would become curable? She wants to cash in those rain checks for the cross-country drive, the European trek, the Alaskan cruise. She wants to retrace her footsteps in Japan, but with Randy. She could introduce Randy to Yoshiko and Fusako. Then they could all find Mr. Inoue and meet the family he was intended to find. She would audit classes just for the hell of it, and she would remember every aspect.

The rain checks specify that I have the ability to fully engage and remember it all.

I never thought that money was important. Experiences and love are better than stuff. But one day I woke up and realized that my life was and always will be paycheck to paycheck. Unlike Michael J. Fox, I will never have a staff, or a foundation, and I realize that having both or even one, or half of one, or one one-thousandth of one, would make what's coming more bearable.

One day I woke up and realized that I have never won anything. Not even bingo. I don't think I am cursed. Perhaps its lack of luck, or not manifesting dreams correctly.

A constipated chokra. A learning disability within my soul. When I see emaciated old men sitting on cardboard boxes by the gas station, I wonder if they are 30-year-old HD people and think how easily it could be me. Some unexpected challenge could rip my white knuckles wide open.

I will never turn down any sage burning in my periphery. And I am wide awake.

Here are more HD fortune cookie messages (insert one per cookie):

Just because I pour my heart out doesn't make me any different from you.

Just because I write about it doesn't mean I get rid of it.

Just because I cry a lot doesn't make me weak.

Just because my words run together doesn't mean that my thoughts aren't clear.

Just because I don't remember you doesn't mean I am gullible.

Just because you share my blood doesn't mean I'll ever let you attack me again.

Just because you "knew me when" doesn't mean you know me now.

Just because I can't answer your question doesn't mean that I've failed.

Just because I agree with you doesn't mean I'm in your pocket.

Just because I forget something doesn't mean I never knew it.

Just because my brain cells are dying doesn't mean I can be brainwashed.

Just because I like you doesn't mean I only like who you like.

Just because I wake up in a nightmare doesn't mean I can't love all the people in it.

And furthermore . . .

Just as I will no longer flog myself because I weigh more than other people, I'm finished feeling guilty for not wanting to do things. It's what the disease is telling me to do. Sitting in my house looking out the window is no tragedy for me. I am quite comfortable and it keeps me safer than messing around in the kitchen where only yesterday I microwaved a jar of peanut butter with metal in it.

The best I can do is good enough. Each day, the best I can do shrinks but gone is the need to apologize for it. There's really no reason to hold on to any of that. There never was.

I excise my shame from Huntington's disease. My ancestors and I are not morally flawed.

I'm letting go of the perception that HD's stigma is equal in intensity to that of a sexual offender.

I am letting me be the me I am becoming and giving that new Sarah a break. Perhaps I can apply some Newcomers club activities for her.

The destination is beyond all of the fear, disappointment, and heartbreak. It's where good days are possible.

Loyalty has many meanings

I feel unconditional positive regard for people who I am friends with. Forever and ever. Many of those friends have cut their losses with me over the years, starting as early as I can remember.

Those who rescue the discarded me eventually feel their lives derailed by my train wreck of a disease. They bail or they fade silently into the background, mistaking the latter approach to be the humane one. What is left of my brain thinks that people are entitled to the lives they want.

But dementia and perseveration lead me to dwell on the bad decisions I have made. I've found that sorry quickly lost its traction. So now at age 59, why don't give not give up feeling sorry. Instead, I should acknowledge that whatever custom calamity HD flings at me as bearable, temporary and most of all, not my intention. It will continue the challenging pattern long past my window of being able to explain it. And I can live with it because that's how the mutation manifests.

I'm not (yet) being invaded by some unknown threat. HD never was a monster, I have learned.

Fear of HD is. I can work with that.

On mornings I wake up and think the test was wrong, I tell myself that it wasn't wrong, and no amount of time travel could change my path.

By now, every function I have is tainted by HD: my sleep, speech, swallowing, moving, thinking and remembering. As HD even permeates my dream life, where an unspoiled yet bitter me may try to wish herself back into existence, I tell her to count some sheep.

My mission is to make life slow down despite my rate of decline speeding up. That calls for mindfulness, meditation, prayer and being outdoors.

Sooner than I think or want, I will reach the place that terrifies me: I will disappear within an operating space that can be understood by nobody.

I can be hypervigilant of my symptoms for troubleshooting purposes, but It's a logical fallacy to think that somehow my damaged brain could or should be in charge of healing itself.

Metaphorically speaking, I need new tools. Instead of using excavators, land movers and concrete, I would do better with feather beds and shiny things. That would be the beginnings of the mental migration necessary to cope.

Stopping my decline is impossible, but I can learn acceptance.

No more thinking that I deserved this because the bitty brigade abhorred the way I coped with the early years of my life.

No more beating myself up for the things that symptoms

bring and take away.

What comes next will depend on reframing the way I experience present tense. That means no comparing my accomplishments to others, especially the multiverse of a million alternate Sarahs who tested negative.

Huntington's disease has always been a part of me. But I am not a mutant. I'm a specialized version of me. It was always just me.

And that must be enough.

That should be OK.

It's time: I forgive myself.

I didn't fuck up or lose.

I was simply born.

THE END

One of these days

One of these days, the cure is gonna come. We'll be following every move. Or it will take us by surprise. At first we won't let our hopes afloat because they've been dashed many times by waves of disappointment. But the cure is gonna come.

Right now, people we will never know are working as if their lives depended on it, racing to cure us. Our babies and us.

They don't sleep much and they know more about HD than we ever want to know. And they're out there now, all over the world, helping us. Our babies and us.

When the cure comes, we rejoice, cry tears of joy for our children and bitter tears for those for whom the cure was too late. There are screams the neighbors can hear, and an internet celebration that will never, ever end. We line up to be saved, and we save all the children first. The ones who suffer now and then the ones at risk.

Then it's our turn. We smile and take a leap of faith through the treatment and into ...

(2020-ish)

Acknowledgments

Thanks to these family members and friends: Blake, Mark, Noah and Rose, Cole, Ezra, Caitlin, Josh and Banks, Ian, John, Dawn and Rainey.

Thank you to Dawn Landau and family and sister Kristen McQuade for the strength of your friendship and support.

Thank you Levonda and Elaine.

Thank you to Michele McMahon. You coaxed me out of the shadows by sharing your own beautiful stories. You inspired me to do the same, and you never stopped reaching out. Thanks for helping facilitate Rupee.

Thanks to Carol and Sam, Mary Etta, Julianne, Kristen, Dawn, Randy and Bob, Teeny, Daphne and Vinod, Sharon and son Randy, Ari and Victoria, Lisa, Taz and Marti, Miki, Paul "Chow," John, D.K. and Jocko and Tom, Laurel Faircloth and the Warrens, Sarah Madru, Jane, Alvis, Jere and Rocky, Dawn B.G., Brian, Anna, Mishelle, Brooke, Sherry, Harold and Mittie, Rebecca W., Kim, Ross and John, Nora, Joanne, Melinda and Wade, Dave, Lavonda, Roxanne, Mable, Jane, Jameesha, Susan, Lorelei Michael B., Morgan, Rose, Dusti, Fred, Vera, Susan C., Matt, CM, Kelly, Andrea, and Jan.